The Other Side *of the* Card

Where Your
Authentic Leadership
Story Begins

MIKE MORRISON

McGraw-Hill

New York   Chicago   San Francisco   Lisbon
London   Madrid   Mexico City   Milan   New Delhi
San Juan   Seoul   Singapore   Sydney   Toronto

The McGraw·Hill Companies

1 2 3 4 5 6 7 8 9 0 DOC/DOC 0 9 8 7 6

ISBN 10: 0-07-147940-6

ISBN 13: 978-0-07-147940-0

McGraw-Hill books are available at special quantity discounts to use as premiums and sales promotions, or for use in corporate training programs. For more information, please write to the Director of Special Sales, Professional Publishing, McGraw-Hill, Two Penn Plaza, New York, NY 10121-2298. Or contact your local bookstore.

Library of Congress Cataloging-in-Publication Data

The other side of the card : the breakthrough method to unleash the leader inside everyone / by Mike Morrison.

    p. cm.

  ISBN 0-07-147940-6 (hardcover : alk. paper) 1. Employees--Coaching of. 2. Leadership. 3. Communication in management. 4. Storytelling. I. Title.

HF5549.5.C53M67 2006

  658.4'092--dc22

                            2006018128

This book is printed on acid-free paper.

For my family, the true source
of meaning in my life.

To my parents, whatever good
I contribute is because of you.

contents

acknowledgments

The people who have been instrumental in helping me to shape my ideas around "meaning" and the central role that it plays in leading come from a wide range of occupations and organizations. Among them are a few people who deserve special recognition—starting with Peter Drucker of Claremont Graduate University. As a Ph.D. student in the 1990s, I had the opportunity to take classes from Peter and collaborate with him on a consulting project for my company. His lectures, mentoring, and writings have had a profound impact on my thinking and the ideas that are presented in this book. It was Peter who first introduced me to the powerful concepts of purpose and their role in driving personal and organizational performance.

I also need to acknowledge Jim Clifton, CEO of The Gallup Organization, for his organization's groundbreaking research in the areas of *strengths theory* (identifying and leveraging our top talents) and *employee engagement* (understanding how a great workplace drives organizational performance). This research has profoundly changed my view of how we need to lead. It has been further enhanced by the unique opportunity to participate with Jim on Gallup's advisory board on positive psychology. The board is helping to chart a new life course that shifts the focus from "what's wrong with us" to how can we organize the abundance of human potential.

Finally, I want to acknowledge all of the wonderful mentors, friends, and family members who serve as irrefutable evidence that leading through meaning is truly the path. A special thanks to those who have made my life meaningful—each with his or her own unique style: Richard Hodge (leading through learning), Mike Downing (leading through others), Thaddeus Smith (leading through personal power), Katz (leading through inquiry), Bryan Bergsteinsson (leading through stewardship), Mike Wells (leading through winning), Dave Harbuck (leading through authenticity), Kelly Aylward (leading through service), Matt Gonzales (leading through insight), Chris Frisina (leading through creativity), Bernie Jaworski (leading through knowledge), Ron Sanchez (leading through faith), my wife Kerry (leading through compassion), and my brother Joe (leading through big ideas).

The role of a corporate leader has evolved more in the last two decades than it has in the preceding two centuries. During the Industrial Age, production efficiency and product uniformity were considered the hallmarks of success. Employees created value for the company by emulating machines; leaders were rewarded for their ability to eliminate variances. Photos of the times glorified the conformity of identically clad assembly line workers and the precise alignment of desks, crossed legs, and hairstyles in vast secretarial pools. Proud and loyal people clung to the hope of lifelong employment while romanticizing the chaos of police precincts and newsrooms.

With the advent of the Information Age, the world turned upside down. The Internet enabled instantaneous communication, invited global competition, and provided a conduit for decentralized decision making. Hierarchies have begun flattening into networks, allowing people to collaborate and share ideas as never before, changing the way people work together—often painfully. The risk of failure has given way to the risk of not experimenting enough and therefore losing market share.

In this blindingly fast paced environment, where nearly every product and service has become a commodity available through multiple channels, how will companies differentiate themselves? How will they remain relevant in the global marketplace?

Today's leading organizations are focusing anew on their values—on who they are and how the work gets done. Their concerns include fair trade, equal employment opportunity, humanitarian labor practices, and ethical governance. They can no longer afford to focus solely on what is delivered. And there's something else.

Leading organizations now realize that they must have a story to tell if they expect to survive. Stories inspire and motivate as no other forms of communications. They have the power to move people to action and find creative new solutions in ways that score-carding variances from the Industrial Age never could.

For most, the story lies in the unique talents, skills, and strengths of people, not in the quality of products, the effectiveness of marketing, or the efficiency of systems. How does a company turn talent into business results? How do you motivate people to innovate and take risks for the greater good of the organization? What kind of culture brings the story alive not only for employees but also for customers, shareholders, and the community?

At Best Buy we envision a "customer-driven, talent-powered" organization in which employees bring their hearts and minds to work as well as their hands. In retailing, where annual turnover among store-level employees typically exceeds 100 percent, this is a radical idea.

But we believe that the way to engage our customers is to fully engage the employees who are closest to the customer, as well as the people who support them at headquarters, in international offices, and in the field. We are determined to understand, appreciate, and deploy the full measure of talent that we have been fortunate enough to attract into our organization. In fact, we must do so in order to continue to innovate, compete, and grow in a global economy.

We understand that the difference between failure and survival (and between mere survival and resounding success) lies in the degree to which our people feel valued and are able to contribute. Creating a culture consistent with our mission, vision, and values is a daunting task for any large company, but we are making progress.

Our first step has been to provide tools for employees to identify their own talents and strengths and to better understand those of others throughout the enterprise. In *The Other Side of the Card*, Morrison's *"me-we"* philosophy emphasizes both the organization's role and the individual's role in feeling fulfilled by one's work and therefore producing outstanding results. (Or as we say at Best Buy, "having fun while being the best.")

The Other Side of the Card is both a simple exercise in self-discovery and a groundbreaking strategy for unleashing hidden talent. Through the story of a CEO's departure from his company and a managers' meeting that changed everything, Morrison skillfully shows how an organization can lose direction when its employees aren't engaged. In the end, of course, the CEO is responsible for reorienting the ship; but first he must ensure that his own vessel is on course.

The anxiety of Morrison's fictional CEO preparing for a life-changing dialogue with managers is palpable. I have often felt the same way! But those discussions must happen or a company misses a rare opportunity to reinvent itself.

This book not only gives executives great ideas to ponder, it also provides an immediate and tangible way to catalyze cultural change within the organization. It is amazing how something as simple as the backside of a business card can help to bring a company's values to life.

Brad Anderson
CEO, Best Buy Co., Inc.

NINETY PERCENT OF THE WORLD'S
WOE COMES FROM PEOPLE NOT
KNOWING THEMSELVES, THEIR
ABILITIES, THEIR FRAILTIES, AND
EVEN THEIR REAL VIRTUES. MOST
OF US GO ALMOST ALL THE WAY
THROUGH LIFE AS COMPLETE
STRANGERS TO OURSELVES.

—Sydney J. Harris

Another leadership book?

My hope is that this one is different. *The Other Side of the Card* focuses on the personal side of leadership where we develop the meaning in our life. This view is not only misunderstood but is rarely developed in our individual lives. Much of the elusiveness of a leading-through-meaning approach is that by its nature it requires that we lean into the failure, pain, insecurity, and negative emotions that represent the critical learning opportunities on our leadership path.

The first part of the journey is inward and represents the path of discovering our personal leadership voice. In finding our voice, we start to see what it truly means to act with integrity. It is not just the positive feelings that are generated when we do what we like to do. It's the wholeness or completeness we feel when we can consistently and deliberately act in alignment with our true self.

Finding our leadership voice is also the process of understanding, aligning, and leveraging our most powerful personal resources. It is the *me* part of the path that is introduced by our main characters in the story that follows. Through them we learn that much of who we are is at an unconscious level or it is buried under the countless adaptations we make to meet the expectations of others.

The second part of the journey—the outer path—is where we find our meaningful place in the world. It is where we come to grips with the most challenging question that life can throw at us: How will I serve others? This journey—the *we* part of the path—is not an easy one. We have to move beyond the dominant pull of our own self-interests. We have to see and integrate others into our lives. We have to develop a way of being that will bring the grit, pluck, and perseverance needed to create meaningful change.

The central reason that few of us leverage our leadership voice is that we fail to develop the personal philosophies that can be articulated to our internal public. In other words, we lack alignment with our selves and thus fail to achieve the personal differentiation developed through the *me* path (I know who I am) and the integration with others achieved through the *we* path (I have found my place in the world). The result is that we can still be good people but we will lack the necessary courage to create meaningful change. Most importantly, we won't have the sense of calling that elevates our status and those we serve.

At first, this practice of developing the personal side of leadership may appear to be too soft or lacking in the practical tactics needed to drive organization performance. But as we dive deeper into the discussion, we will see meaning as the pathway to reaching our true potential as both individuals and organizations. We further discover that creating meaningful change is the central practice of leading and that it provides our best chance to have an extraordinary life within our organizations.

I also must warn you. Integrating these new insights into your life will fully test your personal reflection capabilities. The ability to find the time and space to think—to make ideas our own—has become a lost art in today's go-go world. Many of us seem to go through life without a neutral gear. Through reflection, we learn to view our challenges differently. In this sense, reflection is a key process for shaping meaning in our inner lives—allowing us to engage differently in our outer world. To that end, this book is structured as a personal inquiry.

At the end of each chapter, the reader will have the opportunity to recap:

REVIEW: See a summary of the main learning points.

REFRAME: Consider ideas that represent new ways of thinking.

REFLECT: Engage in thought-provoking questions.

Finally, we will explore the concept of "meaning" through the eyes of a retiring CEO, Seth. His last year has not been an easy one, but through a powerful one-day experience that he leads for the new manager group, he is able to capture for all of us the central truths of leading through meaning.

This book may not be for everyone, but I hope it's for you. I believe it offers an alternate view of leadership—distinguished by a lifetime journey where we seek and create meaning for both ourselves and others.

Let's begin.

At the end of the journey, I lost my way

WHAT DOES NOT DESTROY ME,
MAKES ME STRONGER.

—Friedrich Nietzsche

The retiring CEO of Carlson Packaging Services, Seth Stevens, sat in his office alone. The soft snowfall was a perfect backdrop to support his reflective mood. He was unexpectedly nervous about his upcoming presentation even though he had spoken to this group many times before. It was customary for him, as the senior executive, to set expectations for newly promoted managers within the organization.

But this time it was a little different. This last year leading up to retirement was marked with some unsettling personal revelations. They would have to be reconciled in advance of his presentation.

The last few months also presented some bittersweet moments for Seth because he was saying farewell to an organization that he had driven to success. He knew it would be tough to not come in each day—to lose his connection to something so significant. He was already experiencing the withdrawal pains as his calendar became more ceremonial each day.

For the most part, his role for the last two months morphed into a series of presentations—sort of a victory lap—allowing him to connect with a broad range of fellow associates before moving on to the next chapter in his life.

There were some surprises too. The most significant was the way he was treated due to his outgoing status. It was subtle at first, but it was becoming more and more clear that he was losing his relevancy to the organization. How could this be? After all, he was the one who had guided the organization through its most challenging times! Sure, they were respectful, but they also seemed to look past him.

At first it saddened him. He no longer had the impact he had months earlier when he not only charted the course of the organization but also had great influence over the lives of those in it. He had lost that connection, and now the dutiful deference was being given to a new leader and her team.

As the snow began to pile up on the window ledges, he drifted deeper into his thoughts. The questions kept coming. What is the game that we are playing? How much do we really know and care about each other? How deep are our loyalties to something beyond our own self-interests? The final question was a tough one for Seth: "With all this wonderful success, why do I feel so empty right now?"

He reflected on all the well wishes and promises to "get together" and to "stay in touch." Were these commitments sincere? Or was this just part of the expected corporate patter—the nonsensical way we fill in the pauses and awkward moments that are created by shallow relationships?

Seth also knew that business was a game—and making money was central to winning that game. He gave himself credit for those times as a young CEO when he was able to see the bigger game that existed beyond short-term profitability. It involved playing at a higher level when values and people were engaged.

But Seth also learned that the market could be a dispassionate fellow as it was when Carlson experienced its first major downturn approximately three years ago. For months, the company was in survival mode as sales and profits dropped significantly. Cost cutting had taken some areas down to the bone, significantly eroding the employee loyalty that had been a hallmark of organizational life. Layoffs had become a necessary evil for the first time in Carlson's history—creating high levels of anxiety, vulnerability, and fear in the culture.

For Seth personally, things were also different during this survival phase. The *me-we* philosophy, which had become the foundation for his leadership voice, had fallen to back burner status. In its place was the daily challenge of managing multiple roles—each with its own unique, demanding expectations. Shareholders wanted the emotionless financial manager who could drive results. His leadership team needed a strong rudder to make them feel more secure in their own demanding roles.

He met the challenge. It was amazing how he could switch gears on the run—speaking forcefully to a shareholder group in one instance and then listening empathetically to a troubled colleague in another. But the chameleon-like lifestyle had a cost.

The truth was that it took huge amounts of psychic energy to continually adapt oneself to the external demands of the business. In the darkest moments, it often felt as if his life were not his own. Seth had also lost the sense of authenticity that had characterized his early career.

It would have been easy to rationalize away the guilt. The game had changed. Carlson was swimming in a much bigger pond—almost 30 times larger than when Seth entered the company and 100 times more challenging. The other reality was that Seth simply did not have a lot of options. There just wasn't much slack in the new global economy where even the best had to survive on razor-thin margins. As a result, Carlson faced the cost reductions and layoffs that became inevitable when sales dropped significantly.

Despite the enormous challenges, Seth made it work—ultimately leading Carlson to recovery. But as he moved away from the daily grind, he couldn't help but reflect on the questions that seemed to come from deep within. Why did he lose touch with the *me-we* philosophy that had served him so well throughout his career? How did he let Carlson move away from its customer service culture to focusing relentlessly on meeting the number? How did he lose sight of the bigger game and the opportunities to create real meaning for all the stakeholders? But now the madness was over. Why couldn't he let go?

Seth was brooding now. He had to interrupt this downward spiral of self-talk. There was also an urgency building behind his upcoming orientation for the new managers. It was becoming more and more clear that his message to these future leaders would focus on the deeper and sometimes painful lessons he had learned in his career. He needed to capture these insights in a clear message—one that could not be ignored.

He experimented with some ideas—but as he wrote them out, they seemed like lofty principles with not much behind them. It was the kind of stuff he disdained as a hands-on leader. As he searched for inspiration, he fiddled with the mementos on his desk. One of the items was a gold-plated business card holder with about a dozen cards stacked in place. He grabbed one of the cards.

Seth Stevens
Chief Executive Officer

Carlson Packaging Services

12000 East Riverdale
Lewistown, Illinois   65667
sstevens@carlson.com

Ph: 626-327-7001
Fax: 626-327-7500

He looked at the distinctive lettering. It was impressive. He looked at the title: Chief Executive Officer. He reflected on how it carried a special weight in our culture—with so many aspiring to this distinguishing role at the top. But it never struck him that way. When he was introduced for speeches at external events as the "CEO," he felt somewhat disconnected from the title. At some level it was a source of pride for Seth—but never a source of identity. He realized that this special distinction was never really the goal. It happened as a result of a lot of hard work, but it was never the end he planned for himself.

For some reason, he turned the card over. It was more of an instinctive move—like the automatic way we turn over a coin—or a postcard—to see what is on the other side. It wasn't that he expected anything to be there, but the total blankness brought him to an emotionless stare.

It struck Seth in a peculiar way. For the past couple of hours, in the privacy of his office, he had been looking for meaning. Now, as he held up his business card, he found none. But an idea occurred to him: He would use the other side of the card as his entry point for introducing the powerful *me-we* philosophy to the new manager group.

His mind raced forward. Beyond our achievements, who are we and who will we become? Beyond the job title, what is it that we bring to this job? Beyond the contact information, what do others need to know about us to make a real connection? The ideas flowed as he excitedly built on each new notion. It was clear that the company needed to revitalize its purpose—and the new manager group represented a potentially powerful conduit for achieving that goal.

Now came the tough part of organizing these ideas into a meaningful message. He called his assistant in and quickly reviewed his agenda for the remaining three days of the week. They were full days, but most of the commitments lacked any special significance because he had already turned over power to the incoming CEO.

"Jane, please clear my calendar. I need to prepare for the new manager orientation on Monday." Jane walked out of the office dumfounded. Her boss, Seth, rarely gave this much time to any presentation.

REVIEW

It is failure—not success—that gets most of our attention. Success says everything is OK. Failure sends the signal that something is not right. It is failure that sets the table for learning. Seth, a highly successful CEO by all rational accounts, cannot let go of the perceived failures that now haunt his preretirement life. One question becomes his focus: Why did I lose touch with the *me-we* philosophy that gave so much meaning to my leadership voice?

REFRAME

The other side of the card is our powerful entry point for seeing the blank or undeveloped part of our work lives. It also serves as a useful metaphor for rethinking and responding to the powerful norms that regulate our lives within organizations.

REFLECT

A key part of the leadership journey is developing a sense of self that we are true to. Beyond your achievements, titles, and other accumulations of success, what have you become?

2

At the inn by the lake I cannot rest

I AM NOT BOUND TO WIN, BUT I AM
BOUND TO BE TRUE. I AM NOT
BOUND TO SUCCEED, BUT I AM
BOUND TO LIVE BY THE LIGHT
THAT I HAVE.

—Abraham Lincoln

Instead of coming to the office the next day, Seth made arrangements at the Lakeside Inn that he had routinely visited with his family as a young boy. It was a practice he had carried into his adult life, with the lake now serving as a great place for him to think and create. He was able to reserve the library, which featured a large table and the best view of the lake. Seth walked in with a blank pad of paper and a stack of his business cards.

When he met with the new managers, he would use the business card as a window for seeing one's role differently. It would serve as a simple metaphor for how one-sided our lives can become in organizations. It wouldn't be a speech. It would be more of a discussion about things that matter most—and the role that managers play in relation to those things.

It would also be an opportunity to share personal and sometimes painful lessons learned with the future leaders of the organization. This was an important part of the process for Seth. Things were becoming clearer for him about the real role of managers—especially in developing the other side of the card.

It was not an easy process to do alone. This much think time was challenging for Seth. He was used to the constant interruptions and continuous flow of his CEO life. He actually liked the "busyness" in business. The unstructured time at the lake was difficult to manage. A half dozen times during the day he had to take a break—a short walk, a call home—anything to give his brain a rest. By 4 p.m. on the first day, he was mentally drained.

He looked back through his notes, and his heart began to sink. In review, it was clear that all of the important messages were reduced to bullet points on an agenda or were trivialized in a meaningless training exercise. The powerful meanings of the *me-we* journey got reduced to the remedial rehash of ideas that characterizes most manager training. This would not work. The process needed to be rebuilt around the original intentions. But it would have to wait for now—Seth was in need of a break.

After a short walk and a light supper, Seth settled into a chair for a positive escape into a history novel with just over fifty pages remaining. After rereading the same page three times, he knew that his mind could not focus beyond the mission at hand. He realized he was preparing for much more than a managers orientation. Deep down, he knew that he was struggling to make sense of a career—searching for the meaning that would allow him to finally let go and move into the next phase of his life.

It was approaching 8 p.m. as he grabbed his notes and headed to the inn's library for a cup of tea and more work. He pursed his lips slightly as he reflected on the conundrum he faced. He could be at home with his wife, watching the late night news, which was part of their end-of-the-day routine. Instead, he was struggling with lofty concepts and ideas for small group exercises.

To make the day meaningful for the managers, they would have to make real progress in defining what would go on the other side of their card. Seth hoped that the two perspectives captured by these two simple words—*me* and *we*—would go a long way to completing the identity that was only partially revealed by the face of the card. He grabbed one of his own cards. He turned it over to its blank side and divided it into two equal sections. In each section he wrote one of the two perspectives. There was a simple elegance to the words.

To bring them to life was not as simple as he thought. His previous attempts earlier in the day seemed to trivialize the *me* and *we* paths. Increasingly, his mission became clearer. The new managers would have to experience the *me-we* journey that had been central to Seth's development as a leader.

The next few hours disappeared quickly as the specific steps of the *me* and *we* paths began to emerge. It was exciting for Seth to see his lifelong leadership philosophy translate into a meaningful framework that could be shared with these new managers.

The guiding *me-we* philosophy that changed his life was actually gaining clarity and focus as he tried to make it accessible to others. It was midnight now, and he was tired in a good way—feeling more secure about his content for the meeting. As he gathered his materials he was struck by the realization that you really don't own something until you have to teach it to others.

The next two days went fast as he found a comfortable work rhythm. He learned that he could go about forty-five to fifty minutes before needing some kind of diversion. With a short break, he could throw himself back into his work with a renewed spirit. The new design would put Seth in the middle of a collaborative circle, where storytelling, not computer-driven slides, would serve their need to know.

For Seth, however, this type of meeting format triggered some feelings of vulnerability. Would he be perceived as weak by not making a forceful and compelling presentation from the front of the room? Would he be able to facilitate this type of open discussion? More importantly, would they get it? Would they understand the *me-we* paths that represent the other side of the card, seeing clearly how they connect to their personal and business success?

Seth pulled his notes together and placed them in his oversized portfolio. He then took one last walk around the lake. It was the place of many of his boyhood memories—including his first kiss. With each step he drew power from the deep blue pool that symbolized both the meaning and mystery in his life. He was ready—but there was one more visit he had to make before the big day.

THE MENTOR

It was a beautiful Saturday afternoon as Seth pulled up in front of the simple but well-kept home in one of the local neighborhoods. As expected, Paul Jordan promptly appeared at the door. He had just turned seventy-eight, but he looked much younger. He hustled down the driveway to shake Seth's hand. "So glad to see you, Seth," he remarked. Seth put his arm around his former eighth-grade algebra teacher as they made their way back to the house.

Seth apologized for not keeping in touch. It must have been seven or eight years since he saw Paul Jordan. In fact, he thought it was probably at Ann Jordan's funeral—Paul's wife of forty-seven years. After catching up a little, Paul teasingly pressed Seth for his agenda: "OK, what brings an important executive over to my humble abode? You're not still mad about that 'B' I gave you?"

Seth joined the repartee: "No, although I have never forgiven you, I'm here for a different reason. I wanted you to know that I'm bringing your *me-we* journey to our new managers. I want to do for them what you did for me forty years ago. I know this is a last-minute request, but I would love it if you could join me for at least part of the time on Monday. I want these young managers to meet the man behind these ideas and my life-long mentor."

Paul was deeply moved by the gesture: "Seth, I'll be there. It is probably the most important lesson these new managers can learn." Paul was talking from deep experience. As a young teacher, he developed the *me-we* philosophy as a simple way to promote the most important lesson he had learned in his life. It initially struck him as ironic that a math teacher would find himself immersed in the questions of developing human potential. But over time, the *me-we* philosophy became deeply integrated into this teaching and his life.

"Paul, this session with the new managers will be a challenging one for me. Business has been tough this last decade. To be honest, I think we lost our way. Believe me, as the captain of the ship, this is not easy for me to say. Our purpose has been reduced to surviving in a cutthroat market.

"Don't get me wrong, we have a lot of great people, but the culture is not where it needs to be. We've lost the customer service ethic that once differentiated us. This time the new manager orientation needs to be profoundly different. Instead of focusing on what they need to do as managers, I want to challenge them to lead themselves and Carlson in a more purposeful way. I want them to make the journey from *me* to *we*."

Paul nodded in support and gave Seth a confirming smile. The breakthrough *me-we* discussion between Seth and Paul occurred early in Seth's career with Carlson. But the lifelong mentoring relationship had started more than ten years earlier when Seth was entering eighth grade.

Up until entering Mr. Jordan's homeroom class that year, Seth had struggled in school. As a "repeater" of third grade, he lived with the special shame of having to stay back while all of his friends moved forward. His third grade teacher did all she could to take away the hurt and the sting. Ms. Rachel had been his favorite teacher, and his parents thought it best if she broke the news.

Seth's long walk home from that tearful meeting is still firmly embedded in his psyche. A million questions remained unanswered. Could repeaters go to college? Would he always be behind? Would he always feel this way? Even later in life as a successful executive, it was hard to imagine a deeper sense of failure.

Five years later, Mr. Jordan broke that cycle of doom. Seth noticed right away there was something different. Unlike the other teachers, there was a relaxed nature about him. Seth remembers walking in the first day, and Mr. Jordan was smiling, shaking hands, and engaging effortlessly with the kids. And most surprisingly, he seemed truly interested in the students. There wasn't that typical psychological distance between teacher and student that was the common experience for middle-schoolers.

He started the class by bestowing an A on each student. He made it clear: "What you end up with is up to you. But I believe you are all capable of A work, and my goal as your teacher is to not only expect the best from you but to help you get there."

Seth and his friends held court immediately after the first class and decided that this kind of behavior could not last for long. They were wrong. It became increasingly clear that Mr. Jordan was a great teacher. He made things simple. Each type of problem was carefully broken down into small, comprehensible steps that made the "how" come to life. He also made things interesting. Each type of problem was supported by a learning principle—the "why" behind it—with lots of real-life examples.

To accelerate the learning, there were plenty of challenging quizzes to test progress and promote understanding. But to ensure that the learning did not turn into anxiety, the grade on the quiz did not count unless you wanted it to. Unbelievable! They also got to score their own quizzes, promoting the kind of trust that was rare in the middle school environment. Homework was also on the honor system, but Mr. Jordan continuously encouraged them with his three P's: "Math requires practice, patience, and persistence. Do your homework!"

Later in life Seth came to realize that Mr. Jordan's success was less about teaching math and more about the strong connections he made with his students. It was hard to explain for Seth, but he felt that Mr. Jordan actually saw him as a real person—not just another student he had to tolerate for a year. For three days a week, Mr. Jordan held his "lunch bunch" where kids could get extra help, have fun with a math teaser, or just hang out. Seth never missed a session.

Paul Jordan was also fond of giving kids a special name. It was a way to show that he could see their uniqueness. It also created a special door to enter their young lives. Seth, because of his love for sports, was called "Jack Armstrong, All-American boy." Seth loved the distinction and the attention. In the end, the results for Seth represented a breakthrough, and he moved from a low 'C' to a solid 'B'. Not surprisingly, that same success transferred to all of his classes as Seth started to think of himself differently.

Given the development of this special relationship, it wasn't surprising that Seth kept in touch with Mr. Jordan throughout high school. It was not unusual for his former teacher to come watch Seth's sporting events. Although Seth would occasionally lose contact during the academic part of his college years, he always reclaimed this special relationship during the summer when he returned home.

Over forty years later, the mentor and mentee had now joined forces in a very special way. Just the thought of having Paul in the room on Monday was inspiring to Seth. They spent the next hour going over the flow of events. Finally Seth looked over to Paul and said, "This is going to be cool." Paul smiled and affirmed, "Yes, cool."

REVIEW

Seth is using the managers' orientation as a way to reclaim his leadership voice by helping new managers develop theirs. To make the day meaningful, the managers would have to make real progress in defining what would go on the other side of their card. The other side of the card would symbolize the *me-we* journey—the most important journey we make in life.

REFRAME

The traditional education format would simply not serve Seth's purpose with the new manager group. He could not "train them" on how to develop their unique leadership voice. The day would be built around a self-discovery process that allowed each manager to experience the uniqueness of his or her *me-we* journey.

REFLECT

Most leaders can point to a previous failure or a difficult period in their lives that still serves as a positive catalyst for personal growth and discovery. What is yours? And who helped you through?

chapter 3

One side of the card has writing, the other has meaning

TRUTH IS NOT INTRODUCED TO THE
INDIVIDUAL FROM WITHOUT, BUT
WAS WITHIN HIM ALL THE TIME.

—Søren Kierkegaard

The big day arrived. Thirty-two new managers filed in, and Seth could read them like a book. They were not yet comfortable in their new "manager" skin. Some compensated by overengaging with others—acting as if they had been here before. Others tried to find comfort in a private conversation with a peer—inwardly hoping that nothing in the day's process would expose them. Seth recognized the insecurity and smiled to himself.

He had provided all of the participants with an agenda to give them a way to track progress during the day. However, he purposely did not review any of the content as the session opened. This was to ensure that he did not reveal any of the special tension points that would make up each of the six steps of the *me-we* journey.

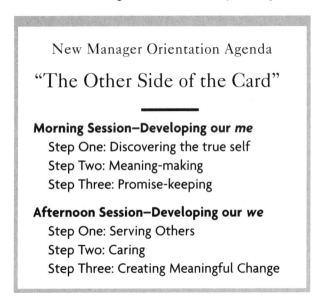

New Manager Orientation Agenda

"The Other Side of the Card"

Morning Session—Developing our *me*
    Step One: Discovering the true self
    Step Two: Meaning-making
    Step Three: Promise-keeping

Afternoon Session—Developing our *we*
    Step One: Serving Others
    Step Two: Caring
    Step Three: Creating Meaningful Change

The last people took their seats, and then all eyes were dutifully on Seth. He paused and took in each face as he looked around the circle. "Welcome all. Let me start by introducing to you a very special guest. His name is Paul Jordan. He was my eighth-grade math teacher who became my mentor—and is now my friend. I have asked him to come here today to help facilitate what I believe to be our most important leadership lessons.

"Now, you have to be asking yourselves, what could I possibly learn about leadership from an eighth-grade math teacher? The answer is—plenty! At the age of thirteen, he put my life on a different course. To describe him as an outstanding math teacher would only capture a small part of his contribution to his students. His real accomplishment involved directing people to the *me-we* journey. Let's give him a warm welcome." Paul beamed as the class gave a strong and affirming applause.

Seth continued, "I know you thought you were coming to a new manager orientation—where I would recognize your new status with some appropriate congratulations and set some expectations around your new role as manager. That is still the plan. But here's the deal. The conversation will be much different from the one I typically have with the new manager group."

Seth paused and provided a quizzical look. "Now this raises an interesting question: What has changed that would warrant such a different discussion?" The group looked around the room with puzzled looks—trying not to make eye contact with Seth. "Let me bring some clarity to the question—with some more questions. Bear with me.

"Between now and two years ago, I want to know if things have gotten better or worse for you. So, here goes. Let's start with complexity. Does life feel more or less complex than it did two years ago?" The simple question launched a spontaneous reaction in the room that included gasps and muffled laughter. "It looks like I touched a nerve. But let me see the hands. How many would say more complex?" Almost all of the hands went up. Seth nodded approvingly.

"OK, next question. How about time? Do you feel that you have more or less time than you did two years ago?" Again, the room experienced a brief eruption of controlled outbursts. Seth could see that they were engaged. "Hands please. How many feel they have less time?" Again, most of the hands went up.

"OK, now let's focus on resources. By *resources*, I mean anything you need to do your jobs. Is there the sense that you have more or less resources than you did two years ago? How many think they have less?" Once again, the vast majority of hands went up amidst the infectious chatter. Seth joined the fun, "I see a pattern here! All right, just two more questions.

"How about expectations on your performance. Have they gone up or down? Obviously, they have gone up big-time in your new roles. But even before the pro-motion, I bet most of you would have answered affir-matively. Am I right?" Seth was greeted with a room of enthusiastic responses and nodding heads.

"Here's the final question. How about work-life balance?" Seth played to the crowd with some humor, "How would you know about something that you have never experienced. I'm not even going to collect your votes!" Seth had them now. "You see where I'm going? How could things be getting worse? Anybody have any ideas?"

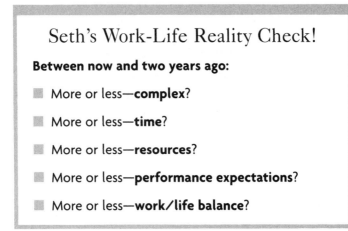

The managers threw out a couple of ideas, but Seth wanted to press them deeper. "Will it get better? In other words, if I show up two years from now, will things have improved? How many think that you will answer the questions in approximately the same way?" Most of the hands were raised. "Now that's a conundrum!

"We should be learning and growing. But for some reason we don't think things will get better. Why is that?" Seth inserted a long dramatic pause as he surveyed the room. "What is the feeling that we get when we sense that things are not getting better and the future is unclear?"

After a few moments of silence, a manager responded, "Feelings of anxiety." Seth jumped forward. "Precisely! Anxiety. It can cover us like a wet blanket—feeling anxious throughout the day—knowing in the back of our minds that things are not getting better. We actually fuel these feelings with our hectic, contemporary lifestyles. We simply maintain a level of busyness that is not healthy.

"I think you know what I mean. Busyness gives us a sense of self-importance. Look how busy I am! Unfortunately, it also relieves us of our need to do the more profound work that will truly make a difference in our personal and professional lives. We can't stop, look, or listen. We are simply too busy going to meetings, saying yes to all requests, and doing our best to keep our heads above water.

"In the process, we begin to lose sight of the bigger things that underlie our work. We continuously attack the surface issues—failing to solve the real root causes of the problems we face. Our bias for action is so strong that we no longer question—why are we even doing this? After a while, we lose the ability to slow down and actually think! In fact, the urgency is to do even more.

"The typical remedy is the time management approach. In other words, we respond to this helpless feeling by trying to manage our time better. We seem to believe that if we could just regain control of our time we could deal with the increasing complexity, reduced resources, and growing expectations. But here's the reality—efficiency is the wrong target! It doesn't help us resolve the real issue of living in a more purposeful way.

"The other reason for this anxiety is also the biggest. It is what psychologists and philosophers call *existential angst*." Seth exaggerated a puzzled look for the audience. "That's too big of a concept for me too. I call it *not knowing who you are*. Here's what I mean. Until we can get clarity on our meanings in life, we will not be able to escape the feelings of anxiety, vulnerability, and frustration that come with our contemporary lifestyles.

"We've all been there. Paul and I will tell you our stories for finding purpose and meaning in our lives and the impact that it has had on others. In the process, we will reveal the *me-we* journey that can serve as a useful guide along the way.

"Before we tell our stories, I want to give you a window to view them through. This window represents one of the most well known business artifacts in the world. Through this artifact we view our organizational lives. In fact, it is the most prevalent medium in the business world. In a moment it can convey status—but at the same time can obscure our true identity, our purpose, and our greatest personal resources.

"More than anything else it symbolizes the game we play in organizational life. It is the central element of the most practiced business protocol in the world. It also represents an opportunity to dramatically reframe one of the most powerful organizing elements of organizational life. We all have one. Actually, hundreds of them! What am I talking about?" Seth paused for a few long moments. "Give up?" The buzz in the room heightened as they searched each other for the answer.

"It is the business card!" Spontaneous chatter erupted. "Please take one out." They all fumbled for a card as Seth pressed them to quickly produce one. "Title? Impressive. Wow, a manager. You have arrived." They enjoyed the good-natured kidding from Seth.

"Company? Very prestigious. Contact information? Fax, phone, e-mail, and cell! Wow, you must be important. OK, now what's on the other side?

Diane Gonzalez
Manager, Customer Services

Carlson Packaging Services

12000 East Riverdale
Lewistown, Illinois   65667
dgonzalez@carlson.com

Ph: 626-327-7347
Fax: 626-327-7554

"Blank you say?" Seth paused and let the question sink in. "That's the part we need to fill in. It's the rest of you that is not captured by your new manager title. It is what our organization needs the most. It is what the world needs the most! But for now, it is blank.

"So, what is on the other side of your card? You say nothing, but I say: I see a master of persuasion who has more patience than Mother Teresa. I ask again: What do you see? You say: Oh, I get it. It's all the stuff that's not on the printed side of the card. I see someone who is underutilized! I say: Good, you do get it. But let's start from the top. Take a good look at your card.

"I see your job title, which represents your current work—but what is your life's work? I also see your contact information. I can now reach you 24/7, but what's the best way for me to connect with you? I see your organization information. I now know who you work for—but whom do you serve?

"These are the questions we will try to answer as we explore the *me-we* path. If you define your life by your career, you will be living too small. If you identify too much with your new manager mask, your energy will be lost meeting external expectations. Paul and I see a different, more challenging path where one learns to find and live out of his or her own unique center.

"On the blank side of your card, please draw a line down the middle. In the left box, write the word *me*. In the right box, write the word *we*. We will begin with what I hope to be our life-changing discoveries on the *me* path."

Me / We

REVIEW

Busyness has replaced purposefulness in our work lives. Although it gives us a sense of self-importance, being busy relieves us of our need to do our most important work. We are simply too busy going to meetings, saying yes to all requests, and doing our best to keep our heads above water. In the process, we begin to lose sight of the bigger things that underlie our work. The *me* path represents the necessary journey for developing a personal and purposeful leadership voice.

REFRAME

Our jobs, and the career tracks that extend them, represent ready-made identities that we can throw ourselves at. Promotions and performance awards propel us forward on the success path. However, if we define our lives by our careers (the printed side of the card), we will be living too small. Our true selves will get lost in the smaller game where meaning is external to us—to be found in a new job or promotion. The other side of the card symbolizes the potential for positive change.

REFLECT

What is the level of anxiety that follows you through the day? To help you answer, complete the exercise that Seth led the managers through. Regarding your work life, between now and two years ago:

- More or less—complexity?
- More or less—time?
- More or less—resources?
- More or less—performance expectations?
- More or less—work life balance?

More importantly, will it be better two years from now?

chapter 4

It was a lie
I told myself

NONE OF US WILL EVER
ACCOMPLISH ANYTHING EXCELLENT
OR COMMANDING EXCEPT WHEN HE
LISTENS TO THIS WHISPER WHICH
IS HEARD BY HIM ALONE.

—Ralph Waldo Emerson

"It's time for the storytelling. It is important that you see the *me-we* journey from the context of a real life. I don't believe it will make any sense to you if I try to explain it any other way. Believe me, all of my efforts to translate what I have learned from Paul into a training program failed miserably.

"Let me do a little set-up for Paul to put things in context. After graduating from college, I returned to Lewistown to begin work. About two years after starting the job, I ran into Mr. Jordan, or Paul, in one of the downtown shops. I was way overdue for a visit anyway. For a few minutes, we engaged in some friendly banter. Then Paul asked if I had eaten yet. I had not—so off we went to the local diner. What happened over the next few hours was truly amazing.

"Paul quickly summoned the waitress and got our orders out of the way. Then he dove right in. He asked a lot of questions about college, favorite courses, new friends, my recent engagement to a local girl, and—of course—my new job with Carlson. The questioning was purposeful, as if Paul had a clear agenda in mind.

"I certainly enjoyed the discussion—after all, it was all about me. As kind of a throwaway comment between bites, I said, 'Things are great.' I'll never forget what happened next. Paul looked me right in the eye in the most penetrating way—as if he were able to look deep inside. He asked, 'Really?' There was an awkward pause for both of us. The friendly discussion had now taken a deliberate turn. Finally Paul broke the silence and said, 'I get a sense that something is missing, Seth.'

"I could not reply at first, but I knew exactly what he meant. It was hard to define, but there was something missing. But was it that obvious? How could Paul see it so clearly? How about others, could they see too?

"I tried a few feeble responses about being a young person and getting my life on track. But I was talking around the real issue. The reality was that I was struggling at work, and it was affecting me in ways that were hard to see. As we continued to talk, insights started to pop into my head. Just talking about it helped. One of the things I revealed to Paul was that sometimes I found myself acting in ways that were not true to myself. It seemed like we were all in a game to please the boss—and impress each other.

"As I talked, Paul would lean in and not say a word. His intentional silence drew me out even more. Our discussion led me to the sobering truth that I was spending a lot of time being someone I was not. And I wasn't quite sure if I was in the right job. I was telling myself to be patient, but I was spending most of my time on these boring planning projects that seemed to go nowhere.

"Paul then let me in on what he already knew. What he saw in me—that something-is-missing look—is what he had seen in himself as a new teacher. So he told me his story. Because his story is also the first story of the *me-we* journey, I am going to ask him to retell the story for you right now. Paul, the floor is yours." Supportive applause filled the room as Paul rose to his feet.

"Thanks, Seth. Thank you all. I'm a little nervous speaking to such a distinguished group." Paul paused briefly and continued, "Here's my *me* story. However, at the end of it, I need to make a confession. But it is best if I save it until then." A sense of intrigue now captured the room as Paul took a few steps forward.

"My story begins during my first year of teaching. Things were going pretty well, but I was still finding my way and making all of the beginner mistakes. But I loved math, and teaching it to kids was a natural thing for me.

"However, I had a friend who at the same time was wildly successful in the real estate market. Like me, Bernie had just started his job, but in his second month on the job he made a commission on a house sale that represented more than I would make in a whole year. I couldn't stand it. He was buying a new car, and I was buying new tires for the tired old one I had inherited from the family.

"Before I knew it, I was studying for the real estate exam and planning my early exit from the teaching profession. Even though it didn't quite feel right, I pushed ahead, and at the end of my first year, I resigned my post. The principal of my school tried her best to talk me out of it, but I was intent on starting the journey to freedom and wealth. Bernie and I were great at dreaming up these wild visions of success. We were drunk with expectation!

"I was not prepared for what happened next. The market tightened a little—and I began to struggle. I kept telling myself to hang in there. I began to think that there was something wrong with me. Bernie was still making deals, and I couldn't get anything to happen. I was working weekends doing cold calls and prospecting. I had no life and was making just enough money to scrape by.

"It took a while, but I finally started being honest with myself. The first truth was that I didn't like the work. In fact, I didn't like any part of the sales process. Bernie saw it as a necessary part of the game to getting all the good things in life. For a while, I pretended that I could work it out—that it would just take more hard work. I put a happy face on it, ensuring family, Bernie, and friends that I was in it for the long haul. But it was a lie. I remember the day I came home and just laid on my kitchen floor and sobbed for an hour. I had hit rock bottom.

"I had also stopped deceiving myself. The sobbing represented my soul's desire to reclaim my life. In that one evening I broke through layers of rationalizations and excuses. I was starting to see clearly that I am first a mathematician and secondly a teacher. Because I was doing neither, my life was increasingly filled with angst." The participants hung on every word as Paul brought increasing emotion to his story.

"It had also become clear to me that I had chosen 'having' over meaning. I had fallen prey to the dominant message of our culture—where the goal is to have. We keep score through our acquisitions and value those who acquire the most. I guess I saw myself gaining prestige and power through having things.

"Lucky for me, a down market kept me from enjoying the success that ultimately could have trapped me. Having things could have won out in my life. But I ended up going back to the meaning path. It is more difficult to see because it is built around experience and not things. Instead of saying 'I have these properties, this income, these advantages,' I would be saying, 'I am a teacher.' The things that mattered most were now within me. 'I have' gave way to 'I create meaning.'

From		To
I		*I*
have		*create*
		meaning

"The next day I mustered all of my courage and walked into the principal's office and bared my soul. I wanted my teaching job back. She truly understood, but she didn't make it easy for me. I would have to start off as a substitute and demonstrate my commitment to teaching. I would have to work my way back to full-time status when an opening occurred. That worked for me.

"I threw myself at every opportunity to substitute—making the most of every teaching moment. Living life for the second time touches the soul in a special way, and I could feel that I was beginning to define the real me at a very deep level. I was more and more confident about reclaiming my uniqueness—my passions for math and teaching. I was ready to put my identity on the line. And that felt good.

"Here's what I learned—we simply cannot be happy in life unless we can find meaning in what we do. It's different for each of us. I love the precision of math.

There's a simple, underlying logic to it that I can get lost in. I am so passionate about math that I want to share it—actually, I have to share it. I guess that's why I gravitated toward teaching instead of engineering. It was the right choice—maybe not from a financial point of view—but it has given my life great purpose.

"Experience has taught me that the starting point for an extraordinary life begins with a strong sense of self. But we just don't wake up one day and find our true selves. It's a process that requires maturity, persistence, and learning. And in my case—a few mistakes along the way. It's a never-ending conversation we have with ourselves. There's no easy way around it.

"Spending a year in the wrong job showed me the true magnitude of our life choices. More importantly, it showed me what could happen when we don't know the meanings in our life. Without knowing our *me*, we can risk our identities, our self-esteem, and our opportunities to make a real contribution. More and more, I was feeling a special accountability to my true strengths and the things that made me unique. I was proud to say that I was a math teacher.

"However, the profound hopelessness I felt as a real estate agent was still haunting me, helping to stoke my inner fire. That experience made me realize that I could not reduce my role to something safe. I couldn't be average." Paul was at the center of the room now. He rotated on his heels as he quietly turned to catch the momentary gaze of each of the participants.

"I owe you one more thing, right?" They all smiled in response. They were anticipating the confession. "Here is the undeniable truth. When I made the move to real estate, I knew at the time it was the wrong decision." Paul paused and repeated his revelation. "I knew it was the wrong decision. I truly knew—but I wouldn't listen to myself. I truly believed that someone else's life—in this case, my friend Bernie's—could be my life. I wanted his success to be my success. But it doesn't work that way. This realization hit me about two years after returning to my teaching job.

"It actually came to me in the middle of the night. At first I thought it was a dream. Maybe it was. I awoke to an amazing revelation. Some inner voice had finally broken through to say that the right answer had been embedded in my feelings all along. At the time of my decision to leave teaching, I was given a warning. It was a deep sense of guilt—but I suppressed it. I worked around it. I never gave it any air. But deep down, I knew. I knew in my heart that I was deceiving myself. I knew in my heart that I was meant to teach."

REVIEW

The starting point for an extraordinary life begins with a strong sense of self. The *me-we* journey is based on this belief. However, we just don't wake up and find our true selves one day. It's a process that requires maturity, persistence, and learning. It also means confronting our self-deceptions. It's a never-ending conversation we have with ourselves as we struggle and ultimately prevail in knowing our true self.

REFRAME

The dominant life orientation in our contemporary culture is to have. We keep score through our acquisitions and value those who acquire the most. The meaning orientation in life is much more elusive and difficult to see. It is built around meaningful experience—instead of things.

REFLECT

Guilt is one of the most important emotions for a leader. It serves as a significant warning that we may be going against what we know is right or what we know to be true. Where is the guilt in your life, and what are the possible self-deceptions that this emotion is trying to reveal?

chapter 5

What I have does not compare to what I have become

"This is the same story Paul told to me over forty years ago. Believe me, I had lots of questions until he turned the tables and asked me one. It was at once the most simple and most difficult of all questions. I was also expecting it. He asked: 'What is your *me*?' I repeated the question out loud—somehow hoping that hearing the words would bring some insight. The question was simply too big for me at my young age—and knowing the details of his me story didn't seem to help. Plus, my focus was toward my pain.

"I confided in Paul that I was still struggling to find a job that I liked. I believed that if I could just find the right work, it would bring meaning to my life. The truth was that I did not like my job, and I was letting it define my happiness. I believed that the right job would change all of that for me. If you think about it, it is how many of us live our lives. We assume that meaning exists outside of us and that we just have to find it.

"In my case, I had begun to adopt this limiting life view in high school. It was one of the most difficult times in my life. Actually, I think it's tough for all of us—as we move from adolescence to adulthood. I remember thinking that everything would be better if I could find my way into the 'popular' clique. Most schools have one. It's the group that typically includes jocks and cheerleaders. I felt that their acceptance would elevate my status—and bring meaning to my insecure, young life.

"I worked my way in through my success in team sports—which can be a big deal in high school. I earned a place at the lunch table unofficially reserved for the 'pops'—as those we excluded affectionately called us. In the beginning, being in the group was the biggest thing in my life.

"But as time went on, my energy was going into maintaining my membership by wearing the mask that distinguished our group. The mask that we wore bore a persona of cool." Seth paused and demonstrated the facial expression as the group erupted in laughter. "We would show a special loyalty to the members of our group while looking past others as if they didn't exist.

"As I reflect on it, I could feel my face physically change to project a special aloofness. It said to others, 'I know you see me but I can't see you.' Beyond the masks we also had to adhere to some unwritten rules to maintain our good standing. We could only go to a school dance, for example, if the group decided that we could go. In the end, being part of the group did not protect us from the loneliness and despair of young adulthood.

"After high school, the focus shifted onto getting into the right college. In my case, it was the state university. My acceptance provided me with a ready-made identity that I could move into. Now I could find meaning in my life because I was attached to something of significance—in this case the right school." Seth inserted a lengthy pause. "Or so I thought. Unfortunately, that kind of thinking represents the same 'having' versus 'meaning' trap that Paul talked about earlier.

"The 'having' orientation was becoming my way of life. It was about having the best things—having the right friends—having the right degree from the right college. My source of meaning was outside of me. It was a possession. It was also the wrong focus.

"When your life is oriented to having things, even something like education becomes a possession. Here is how it works: Having a degree from the state university meant prestige and greatly improved chances for one of the better jobs after graduation. With an orientation to having the degree, I lost sight of the experience of gaining new knowledge.

"As a result, my focus in school was on scoring well on the tests. Doing well on the tests earned me good grades toward having the prize at the end—the degree. The problem was that the learning experience was not deep enough to enrich me—to become part of me. I owned the new knowledge temporarily in support of my having a degree.

"After I graduated from college, one of my early mentors, Ben, reinforced the having orientation. Since I was moving up in the organization, he thought it would be important to increase my leadership credentials, thereby enhancing my status in the eyes of others. I remember Ben's comments about my résumé looking a little light. So, without much thought, he helped me join two of the local service and community organizations with a view toward getting into visible leadership roles.

"You can see where I'm going with this. My focus was on possessing or having something that would look good on my résumé. As a result, my interest in these organizations was only superficial. While I could take credit on my résumé for playing a leadership role, I gained very little in terms of real leadership experience.

"It doesn't stop there!" Seth made his pronouncement, walked to the board, and wrote down a simple question. He paused, letting the words sink in.

Who are you?

"Seems like the right place to start—to get to our *me*. In fact, it is probably the most asked question in the world. 'Who are you?' Unfortunately, it often leads us back to the having orientation. We tend to answer the question through the lens of a personal résumé. I have these degrees. I have these experiences. I have these accomplishments. That's who I am. I am the sum of these things that I have accumulated. I am my résumé.

"The collecting of accomplishments is continually reinforced by those around us. I wish I had a nickel for every time someone has said to me 'This will look good on your résumé.' You can see how the having orientation can impact us beyond our need to consume and acquire things. We end up having friends without truly knowing them, having a degree without any real lasting knowledge, having a career without developing our true potential, and having all these things that exist outside of us without creating a meaningful life.

"This is a critical pause point—a yellow light representing the need to slow down for one of the most dangerous intersections in our lives. I believe the printed side of our business cards supports the having orientation in life. It is the dominant view. If we are going to have any chance for a meaningful life, we need to define the other side of the card—starting with *me*.

"Paul would not let me off the hook when it came to defining my *me*. I am going to do the same with you. I am going to take you through the same process he took me through—one question at a time. I've added my own ideas, but the process will be true to Paul's original *me-we* journey.

"The main challenge in establishing our me is to shift the dominant having orientation to the meaning orientation. I want you to experience each of the six key steps on the journey today. My hope is that you will be able to repeat these steps after our time together. It starts with step 1, discovering the true self." Seth walked to the flip chart and revealed the following:

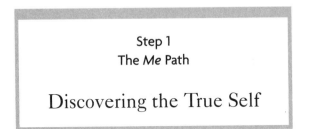

Step 1
The *Me* Path

Discovering the True Self

"We are not a blank slate. We're born with certain gifts and a uniqueness that is symbolized by our unique fingerprints. My mother had the most beautiful voice in the world. Unfortunately I didn't get those genes. They were left out, and no matter how hard I have tried; I simply cannot carry a tune.

"We often see these gifts begin to appear at a very early age. At age two, we could tell that my daughter had some unbelievable physical talents. So it was no surprise to us that she became a scholarship athlete in college. I believe there are things that are deeply embedded within us. One thing embedded in me, for example, is my need to generate new ideas. Inside Paul is his passion for precision. He tried to walk away from it but couldn't do it.

"Our first step on the *me* path is discovering our true self. In small groups of three and four, I want you to answer the following questions." Seth walked to one of his flip charts and turned over the blank page revealing the first step of the *me* path. He read each question out loud.

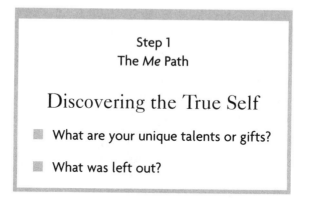

Step 1
The *Me* Path

Discovering the True Self

▓ What are your unique talents or gifts?

▓ What was left out?

"Before we start, I want to share a little about how I answered those questions. It may help you avoid the traps I fell into.

"I must admit that this exercise took some time for me. Thank goodness for Paul's patience. My initial response was that my gifts were in the areas of analysis and problem solving. Actually, that was just some wishful thinking.

"I said those things because I thought they made me look good in the eyes of others. I was always impressed with people who were great at analyzing things. I guess that started in college where those kinds of talents paid off in high GPAs and lots of teacher attention. In reality, I didn't have those talents, but I appreciated them in others to such a high degree that I wanted those qualities to be a part of my public identity.

"Like a good mentor, Paul challenged me on it. He felt I was spending too much time fixated on my weaknesses, and he wanted me to focus on my areas of strength. As we worked through it, it became clear that I was always the one who was good at seeing the bigger picture. I was the creative, strategic one who didn't get frustrated with big concepts. While lots of new ideas may frustrate others, they sustained me.

"Sometimes it got me into a little trouble because I loved to explore new ideas and push the envelope. For my fellow colleagues who were more practical minded, my constant idea generation was a little annoying. They wanted to get their jobs done, and I wanted to reinvent our work. As a new employee, I succeeded in establishing myself as 'having my head in the clouds' and 'lacking focus.' I learned the painful lesson that our strengths, when overused, can also be our weakness.

"But over time, it became more and more clear to me that I was a big-ideas person and these ideas were needed at Carlson. Even though the ideas themselves weren't always appreciated, I grew comfortable with my special role in encouraging divergent thinking. I also loved to make things happen. I would feel great frustration when things weren't progressing—which unfortunately was the normal state of affairs for my first jobs within Carlson. That's a little bit of my true-self story. Now it's time to hear yours. You won't get it all figured out today, but we're going to start the process."

A buzz filled the room as the participants revealed their strengths and weaknesses in the safe environment created by Seth. He led a lively debriefing of the insights gained from the exercise. One participant, Jan, expressed a common sentiment: "We take our strengths for granted. We're much more interested in fixing ourselves—and others." Charles joined in: "I could list my weaknesses—what was left out—right away. I struggled to identify my special talents."

Seth continued: "We could spend a whole day exploring our gifts and the strategies that would leverage them. But instead of continuing, we're going to stop here knowing that you will have a whole lifetime to continue this discovery process. Now that you've begun it, your biggest challenge will be to create the time and space to do it.

"To reach closure for today, take out another business card. On the blank side, give yourself a new title that reflects your true self. Remember, your current job title shows your place in the hierarchy and your role in

the structure. But it doesn't reveal much about you—
especially the unique you.

"My favorite example comes from my assistant,
Jane. Her official title is 'executive assistant,' but her
self-proclaimed, nonofficial title is 'cruise director.' She
loves planning events for the organization, and she is
the one that makes sure that we celebrate all of our vic-
tories along the way. No one ever assigned those
responsibilities to her. From a true-self perspective, it
would be impossible for her to suppress the cruise director that lives within.

"Your turn! Claim a title and put it on the blank side
of your card. You've got two minutes to come up with
one—and when I call time, you have five minutes to
share it with as many of your colleagues as possible!"
The exercise started to reveal the real power in the
room—with Seth capturing some of the names on a flip
chart to keep the energy flowing.

The "Other Side of the Card" Titles

- The Vision-ator
- A Devil for Details
- Once and Done
- Captain Courageous
- Mr. Precision
- Wired for Hire
- Matt the Technocrat
- The Project Meister

REVIEW

The first step on the *me* path is claiming our true self. We are not a blank slate. We're born with certain gifts that make each of us unique, which is symbolized by our unique fingerprints. The pathway to our true effectiveness and happiness is understanding and leveraging those strengths. Until we can do so, we will be destined to live someone else's life. We will want their gifts to be ours—failing to find and develop our own center of power.

REFRAME

The great tragedy in life is our fixation on what is wrong with our selves instead of what is right. What we see first is our weaknesses and the weaknesses of others. To begin the *me-we* journey requires developing a sense of the true self—faithfully acknowledging our strengths and learning to manage around our weaknesses.

REFLECT

First, what is the one unique talent that defines you best, and how can you leverage it more fully as a leader? Second, what title would best capture your irrepressible true self? Finally, what is a weakness that captures too much of your psychic energy?

chapter 6

I lead life; life does not lead me

Seth started to sense that a special feeling had captured many of the participants. He could see it in their body language and hear it in their voices. Hope. Anticipation. Wonder. It buoyed his spirit as he began again: "With a strong sense of our true self, we are ready to take the second step on the *me* path. It's where we learn to translate our experiences into meaning.

"It starts with the belief that there is an overall purpose to life. In other words, we believe there is a bigger game to be played. For some, this purpose is built-in around religious foundations. It is easy to see how religion, with its reliance on service and a relationship with God, plays a key meaning-shaping role in many of our lives.

"For others, a sense of purpose comes from the strong social cues of their culture. I have always been intrigued with how the American culture, with its focus on the individual, is so different from Asian cultures, in which group and community norms tend to be more powerful. In our culture, we tell our kids to be 'all you can be.' In one Asian culture, there is a popular saying that reminds everyone that the nail that sticks up gets hammered down.

"Still for some, their sense of purpose is built around personal values that are learned from significant others and teased out from their own life experience. I can see where all three—religious principles, cultural norms, and personal values—have contributed to the ideas and ideals that are bigger than myself. The belief that there is an overall purpose to life sets the stage for meaning to exist.

"But it is the presence of real problems and challenges that stimulates the meaning-making process. In other words, the process for creating meaning is actually quite natural. The questions that follow a problem are irrepressible." Seth paused and then announced: "A big problem has just occurred in my life!" He then revealed three questions he had written on one of the flip chart pages and read them aloud.

> ▪ What does this *mean* to me?
>
> ▪ What is the *meaningful* thing to do?
>
> ▪ What new *meaning* can I create from this experience?

"If you think about it, Paul responded to all three in his dilemma. For a person of purpose, they are impossible to ignore." Seth revealed a new flip chart page that showed Paul's response to each question.

> ▪ What does this *mean* to me?
>
> "I am in the wrong job and I can't stop kidding myself."
>
> ▪ What is the *meaningful* thing to do?
>
> "I need to return to teaching math – where I can make a difference."
>
> ▪ What new *meaning* can I create from this experience?
>
> "I will commit myself in a special way to helping my students develop confidence in the learning that will follow them into life."

Seth read each one of the responses out loud—adding his own insights to Paul's remarkable story. "As you can see, meaning is a powerful window through which to view life as we live it. For Paul, meaning-making was the pathway for getting his life back on track.

"Let me share another example that brings this point home. Imagine the pain of a mother losing a child to a drunk driver. To me, the loss seems almost unbearable. But amazingly, we see wonderful examples of how the human spirit can prevail." Seth revealed a new flip chart page that showed a mother's possible response to each question.

Again, Seth presented each response to the three questions—showing the central role that meaning plays in dealing with the challenges of life.

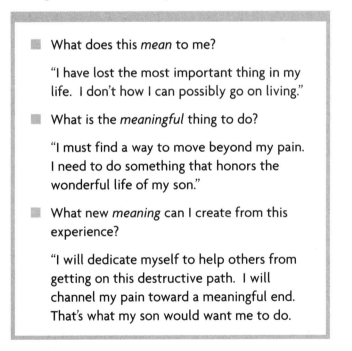

- What does this *mean* to me?

  "I have lost the most important thing in my life. I don't how I can possibly go on living."

- What is the *meaningful* thing to do?

  "I must find a way to move beyond my pain. I need to do something that honors the wonderful life of my son."

- What new *meaning* can I create from this experience?

  "I will dedicate myself to help others from getting on this destructive path. I will channel my pain toward a meaningful end. That's what my son would want me to do.

"As we can see from these examples, life can be difficult—and at times impossible. As you can also see, meaning serves as a source of stability during these challenging times. When we get thrown for a loop, it is natural for us to hunker down and engage in a process that will help us make sense out of what happened. In fact, we have to. It's the only way to move on."

Seth revealed the following page on one of his flip charts. "Now it is your turn at the three questions." Seth read each one out loud. "We have a lot of ground to cover here, so let's answer these questions and share our responses in pairs. Please begin."

Step 2
The *Me* Path

Leveraging the Meaning-Making Process

Identify a key experience in your life that initiated a search for meaning?

1. What did this experience *mean* to you?

2. What was your *meaningful* response?

3. What new *meaning* do you continue to create from this experience?

Seth gave this exercise some time as he monitored the level of engagement. Overall he was impressed with what he saw—a lot of furrowed brows as the participants leaned into their discussions. He finally called time and brought the group back together to share the lessons they had learned in the smaller groups.

He was both surprised and excited about the depth and insight of their responses. Clearly, meaning-making had played an important role in their lives. "First of all, I am truly impressed with this group. But we are not quite done.

"I want to introduce you to two critical capabilities that you will need to make the meaning-making process truly come to life. I learned them from Paul, and I call them 'R&R.' I believe the best way to reveal them to you is through the following story. You all know Angela Thompson, our controller. You also know that she is one of the most loyal and dedicated members of the leadership team. At the midpoint of her career, she was passed over by a candidate of much lesser capability and contribution. Sadly, it was obvious to most—and it created a difficult time for Angela.

"She and I had entered Carlson at about the same time, and we had developed a special friendship as we supported each other through the normal slings and arrows of organizational life. But this was not an easy one. Angela had given so much of her life to Carlson— so it was natural that she felt betrayed.

"The first few days were highly emotional. For the most part, she spent the time planning her departure. She rehearsed her comments that she would make to her boss and others. There was a sense of satisfaction as she practiced explaining the hurt and emotional upheaval that she had gone through. They would see their wrong-doing and be deeply saddened by her leaving. As much as I tried, it seemed impossible for me to offer an alternative view.

"The next few days produced a breakthrough. As much as Angela wanted to express her hurt and seek redemption for the misdeeds against her, deep down she knew this path would not serve her well. As the emotions began to subside, Angela was able to go off-line and begin to reflect. She realized that she had too much invested in her work—and her relationships. She soon came to the clear realization that she could not quit. Through reflection, Angela was able to shift the meaning-making process to a higher game. She had turned the corner.

"This is an important pause point. Reflection is the art of thoughtful thinking—and it is also the first R in R&R. It's what you do when you don't know what to do. Think of it as 'time-out' for adults. We give our kids time-out when we want to slow them down and get them to think about what they just did. When it comes to meaning-making, reflection is the process of slowing down and thinking about what you are going to do. You don't need a mountaintop. You just need to create some time and space.

"Another key element of reflection is that we remain open to adjusting our ideas about our selves and the world. By doing so, we learn to view our challenges differently. It allows us to counter the automatic, impulsive thinking that leads us to the same insights and solutions. It is also a skill that we cultivate over time—especially as meaning begins to play a more central role in our lives. In fact, we simply cannot grow without time to think and learn from our experience. That's exactly what I saw in Angela.

"It was unbelievable to watch as her tone went from total self-absorption to reflective mindfulness. The reality was that she had been passed over by a man of lesser qualifications. That was twenty years ago—and sadly, in our organization it happened more than any of us would have liked to admit. But in the end, Angela felt she owed it to herself and other women to persevere. Deep down she knew that she was instrumental to the gains already achieved by Carlson in creating a level playing field for women. She couldn't call it quits.

"What Angela did next represents the second R in R&R. Angela took a very difficult experience and reframed it in a positive way. This reframing process allowed her to see beyond the injustice to the benefits of staying. If she could not find these meanings, emotions probably would have won out. If she hadn't been able to engage in the meaning-making processes of reflection and reframing, she would not have seen the larger, more meaningful opportunity that ultimately prevailed.

"Here's the amazing thing. To this day, she still believes that being passed over was one of the best things that ever happened to her. That is the role that meaning plays. It not only allows us to make sense out of what happened but it can also enrich our decisions for a lifetime.

"It's your turn for a little R&R. Please take out three business cards. I want you to leave the room and find some quiet space on the grounds. By doing so, I want to reinforce the action of deliberately going off-line to reflect. Coach yourself to be open and flexible as you complete this assignment. As you could see from the Angela example, it is not an easy thing to do. But if you can cultivate your reflection and reframing capabilities, you can dramatically change your life.

"Here's what I want you to do. I call it the 'flip-it exercise.' Try to come up with at least three burdens you are currently carrying. In other words, what are the things that you are feeling guilty about, fretting about, or perhaps repressing because of their negative nature? Maybe one of them is the fact that your mother-in-law will be spending the holiday with you. Or one might be a deteriorating work relationship with a colleague. It doesn't matter. Draw a simple line down the middle of each business card, and write them down in the left column." Seth revealed a blank flip chart page and simply drew a line down the middle.

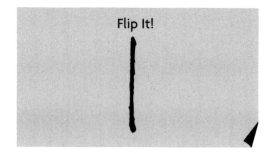

"In the right-hand column, do some reframing or opportunity finding with each of the situations. In others words, flip it. Find the good news in the situation.

While your mother-in-law provides great heartburn to you, your kids love her. That's a benefit. The poor relationship with a colleague represents an opportunity to develop your interpersonal skills. What would be the benefits if you could turn it around?" Seth paused briefly and then added one last instruction. "Truly try to see the good news in each situation. Believe me, it is there. Please begin!"

The exercise was an engaging one. With Seth's encouragement, a participant, Gina, shared one of her examples with the group. "I have been feeling some guilt about not spending enough time with my new baby. It got worse with the likely increase in work due to my new manager position. I flipped it. I am looking at my new role as an opportunity to have more influence over my time—not less. I want to do the same for my new team members and help them achieve work-life balance."

Seth completed the post mortem. "Once you have been successful at turning a negative into something positive, you begin to change your orientation to life. The facts don't change, but how you view them does. Also, not every situation is 'flip-able'—but the ability to see meaning in difficult situations is a wonderful gift that only a few of us will ever own. To engage in meaning-making is to turn on all of your reflective powers and answer simple questions like the ones I posed today."

REVIEW

The second step on the *me* path is meaning-making. It's where we learn to translate our experiences into meaning. The contemporary work life is often filled with feelings of anxiety, vulnerability, and frustration. To a significant degree, these feelings are generated by the dominant having orientation. The only effective response is to use our ability to create meaning. It starts with the belief that there is an overall purpose to life. It is typically fueled by our spiritual life, our culture, or our own conscience. In other words, we believe there is a bigger game to be played. Our desire to be purposeful in life sets the stage—but it is the presence of real problems and challenges that stimulates the meaning-making process.

REFRAME

The two critical capabilities that we will need to make the meaning-making process truly come to life are reflection (the ability to go off-line and think) and reframing (the ability to positively rethink the possibilities). They are foundational to living a meaningful life and developing our leadership voice.

REFLECT

What are some of the burdens that you are carrying that need to be "flipped"—or reframed from negative to positive?

I did the *right* thing instead of the right thing

THE PURPOSE OF LIFE IS A LIFE OF
PURPOSE.

—Robert Byrne

Seth ventured outside of the conference center to find a bench where he could sit and just breathe. He had to turn everything else off, at least for a few minutes. The cold winter air created the perfect stillness for his time-out. Things were going well, but guiding people through a personal self-discovery process was emotionally draining.

It was 11 a.m. now. He had just one more session before lunch, and he wanted to end the morning on a high note. He extended the break a few additional minutes, using the quiet time to get centered for his next presentation. He savored the extra moments.

It was time now to introduce the managers to the third and final step on the *me* path. After corralling them back into their seats, he cautioned them that this step was the most difficult to grasp. The warning seemed to capture their attention.

Seth knew from his own personal experience that the personal values discussion was inherently challenging mostly because values remain hidden, ambiguous, and intangible. That is, until they are tested. In helping to bring those values to the surface, his goal was to build a realistic appreciation for what he knew to be the most powerful force in both personal and organizational life.

The first thing that Seth did was to help these young managers get comfortable with the wide range of personal values at play in their lives. To do this, he had to bring the abstract notion of personal values down to ground level. He revealed a flip chart page with the following definition: "Personal values are the promises we make to our selves and others." His reasoning was simple: If values are the principles that we live by, then they represent the promises we make in life.

Seth had discovered a few years earlier that by substituting the word *promise* for *values,* an elusive discussion of values would move from lofty to pragmatic. He found it almost amusing how his executive team would fumble whenever they tried to bring any coherency in setting and communicating Carlson's "values." At best, the "values" they produced were rambling platitudes. Through frustration and dumb luck, he finally asked: "What are the promises we need to make to our stakeholders?" They got it right away. It was amazing how they were able to articulate their promises to customers, employees, partners, and investors in simple but compelling terms. Seth remembered the first one they completed: "We promise to provide a prompt return on any product or service that does not provide 100 percent satisfaction."

He then asked the present group of new managers to take a clean sheet of paper and try to fill it in with all of the promises they have made to their personal self and others. He cautioned them that many of the promises they were writing today—especially the ones we make to our personal selves—were being articulated for the first time. In other words, they existed as "fuzzy" promises that needed further refinement.

Seth surveyed the room as the managers began to fill their pages. His eyes soon found Linda Terri, whom Seth had been monitoring since the beginning of the day. She had been on senior management's radar screen for a couple of years due to her bulldog tenacity and creativity in developing new products. She had an eye for innovation and she often made things happen by the sheer force of her will.

Seth had begun to develop a relationship with Linda through the various meetings that had brought them together. She would always greet him warmly, and she loved to engage him in some new idea that she had cooking. But today was different.

Her communications with Seth were all too brief and lacked any kind of emotion. Seth knew that something was up. What he didn't know was that Linda had accepted a job with another company. A headhunter had recruited her to a smaller organization that competed with Carlson. She would give her two weeks' notice as soon as she received the official offer letter, which would probably come tomorrow. It felt great to be wanted, and the generous offer seemed almost impossible for Linda to turn down.

Now she was wishing that she had not come today. All of the engaging stories and opportunities for reflection had Linda second-guessing the decision she had made. Seth's story about Angela's "reflecting and reframing" her way to staying at Carlson did the most damage. Linda was starting to ask herself tough questions as she completed the "I promise" exercise shown below. What were the real reasons for wanting to change jobs? Why was her decision in so much doubt? Was it too late to change her mind?

Seth noticed that almost every manager had a full page of entries. It was a good sign that a lot of promises were at play in their lives. He introduced the next key insight on a flip chart: It is through our actions that we begin to understand the real depth of our promises and commitments.

I PROMISE . . .

- To make my family the center of my life

- To be fair and honest in all of my dealings

- To have a friend in God

- To always do my best at work

- To be a good friend to others–worthy of trust

- To take care of my health with the right nutrition and exercise

- To consistently help others who are less fortunate

- To mentor and coach those who seek my guidance and support

- To be a true professional–living up to the responsibility placed in me

- To be a leader of change

- To develop myself and others

- To dedicate time weekly to community service

- To consistently show the virtues of tolerance, love, and faith

Seth explained further: "I may espouse to others my dedication to family, but what does it mean when I always put my work first? We all talk a good game, but the truth lies in our deeds. In fact, many of our promises will not emerge until a key event happens in our lives. Let me give you a personal example."

Personal Values

Personal values are the
promises we make
to ourselves and others

"My son Jonathon was born with a significant hearing defect. The doctors were not optimistic with their early prognosis. He was our first child, and it was devastating news. At first, I pretended that the condition wasn't really there. I had this perfect vision of a son who would be an extension of me—only better. That vision did not include any significant physical limitation. So at first, I suppressed it.

"My courageous wife confronted me early on. She could tell that I wasn't accepting the truth behind Jonathon's condition. Through some painful dialogue I started to acknowledge his physical challenge in a more positive way. Unfortunately, it didn't take me long before I went to the other extreme.

"I became continuously aware of his limitation. It was always the first thing I saw in him. Mostly I was overprotective. I was hyperalert to situations that might expose his weakness. But the truth was that I was treating him as less than whole. It never felt right—but somehow I thought it was the right thing to do.

"One day I was playing with Jonathan at the park. He was about two and a half years old at the time—a real bundle of energy. As we guided his trucks through the sand, it struck me like a ton of bricks. He was totally absorbed in the moment. For him, the hearing defect was not a loss. It was all he knew. It certainly did not get in the way of his ability to play, to show emotion, and to be happy. At that moment, I decided to view Jonathan's challenge the same way he did. I made a commitment to see my son with different eyes. With that simple shift in perspective, I felt a huge weight lift.

"However, it wasn't until later in life that I understood the true significance of this change. Because of advances in medical science in this field, much of Jonathon's hearing loss had been restored over a series of operations, which allowed him to live a fairly normal adolescent life. The day before his high school graduation he came to me to reveal a powerful secret that he had held since age five. He told me that he had been more aware of his hearing handicap then he had let on. Deep down, he knew that he was different from the other kids, and he felt insecure about his ability to make his father proud the way the other kids were making their parents proud of their classroom and athletic accomplishments. The next revelation left me in tears.

"Jonathon told me of a family video clip that featured the two of us when he was about five years old. Together we were building a block set. The scene went for only about eight minutes, but in it he saw that I was totally absorbed in the moment. He could tell by my smile and my genuine actions that my mind wasn't anywhere else—I was focused solely on him and our special activity together.

"It served as proof to him that I loved him and saw beyond his limitations. He said he had replayed it hundreds of times over the last ten years to counter the insecurity that would creep into a life that often felt less than whole. He said there had been many other father-son moments, but this was his favorite—this one always brought him back.

"I was speechless. Because of Jonathan I started to see the real humanness in people. I was able to move away from the unrealistic expectations that make us all look deficient in some way. I got very good at seeing the good news in people. This meaning-making journey has changed my life—and has led to the development of one of my life promises. What emerged was a new *me* that no longer saw the limitations in a physical defect but saw the potential to positively transform all of those involved.

"Over time my *me* became a great advocate—not for the physically challenged but for the human spirit. As a result, my leading question for any person I wanted to develop became quite consistent: 'So, what barriers have you had to overcome? What did you do when they said no to your idea? What is profoundly different about you as a result of your challenges in life?'

"Over time, our *me* becomes a true force. The *me* says I am more than a collection of experiences. I am more than my natural talents. I am grounded in the personal values and promises that I have teased out in my life."

Seth revealed further insights. "These promises represent the foundation upon which we pursue the meaning that we need in our lives. These promises demonstrate to our internal public—our inner selves—the positive nature of our true selves. They provide a sense of stability in the constant sea of change that represents our contemporary lifestyles. They also make us feel significant in a world that hardly seems to notice us."

Seth paused and checked to make sure everyone was still with him. "So far, so good?" He saw heads nodding affirmatively, so he moved on. "By now, you know the drill. This time, however, take out two business cards." Seth gave them a little time to get their cards ready. He then revealed the next assignment on a flip chart page.

Step 3
The *Me* Path
From Meaning-Making to Promise-Keeping

▪ Identify a meaning-making experience or period in your life that led you to **confirm** or **create** a *promise*. Describe it in a few words.

▪ On another card, describe the *promise* in ten words or less.

"From your personal life, think about some of the most important meaning-making experiences or periods in your life. Pick one that led you to confirm or create a new promise. On the blank side of the first card, describe that promise in ten words or less. Now here is the kicker. I want you to claim it.

"This is more than an academic exercise. This is your life! I want you to claim a promise that you truly own and are not afraid to put out there for everyone to see." Seth now held up one of his cards. Written on the back was his personal promise that related to the experience with his son. He read the card out loud: "I promise to see the good news—not the limitations—in people."

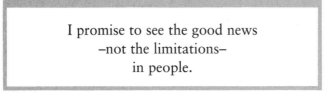

I promise to see the good news
–not the limitations–
in people.

After about twenty minutes, Seth called time and began to debrief the managers. Linda was clearly locked into her own personal post mortem. There was a special urgency to Seth's questions, and she applied herself with a focused determination. Inspired by the stories and insights from Paul and Seth, she was fully engaged in the meaning-making process. She wanted to know the truth. Her reflections now revealed a range of reasons that led her to leave Carlson. She wrote them on the back of one card.

This will be good for my career.

Everyone needs a change.

I'm not fully appreciated here.

I'll be able to do more in a smaller company.

Carlson has gotten too big and impersonal.

The extra money will help.

They really need me at the new company.

I can re-invent myself.

Leaving Carlson appeared to be the right thing to do—but was it the *right* thing to do? Slowly but surely she was beginning to see that these entries on the card were only half-truths—rationalizations that protected her self-deception. On the surface they were true. But Linda was starting to see that she was being pulled along by the newness and excitement of a new opportunity that promised to give new meaning to her life.

She was also admitting to herself that she had fallen into a trap—the same one Paul had fallen into when he left his teaching job. She had given in to the belief that meaning existed outside of her. All she had to do was find it. In this case, it found her. This new job would fill all of the voids in her work life. It would be great. Unfortunately, the morning discussions, stories, and exercises turned that assumption upside down.

THE OTHER SIDE OF THE CARD

The questions kept coming. What is the meaning I bring to this life and to my work? What am I trying to find? If I leave now, what will happen to me? As Linda struggled with each question, she also began to reframe her challenge. She was starting to see the new job opportunity as a test.

It was testing her resolve and commitment to keeping the big promises that she had made to herself and others while at Carlson. As she looked over her "I promise" list, she realized that much of her life and many of her commitments were focused on Carlson and the people in it. She had deep mentoring relationships within Carlson where people were counting on her. She had continually asked for more responsibility and had received it.

This was not easy for Linda—especially because there was the one commitment that she had left off the "I promise" list. Two years ago she had committed herself and her team to winning their industry's most prestigious innovation award for product development. In a matter of weeks, it became a compelling vision for the whole organization—attracting some of the best performers across the company.

The actual award was only a symbol for Linda and her team. They were focused more on the journey that would get them there. They knew it would spur some of the necessary changes to their products and services while developing the relationships among all of those involved. Deep down, Linda knew this was also a promise to herself and others that she would do all in her power to reach this end.

Things certainly were not perfect at Carlson, but increasingly Linda was positioned to make them better. The meaning-making process—the reflection and reframing—had led her to some important new revelations. Her work life was not just an economic transaction where her services would go to the highest bidder.

She had made sizable personal investments in both her work and her coworkers that were much deeper than the expectations of an employment contract. Deep down, she also knew that she had made promises that she would have to keep.

It was also testing her willingness to take full responsibility for developing the meaning in her life— and not letting that meaning fall to something that would lie outside of her. Linda was coming to grips with the reality that she had romanticized the benefits that would come from this new job. In the span of only a moment, it all became clear. It was an epiphany of sorts. She could not—she would not—leave. The back of her card read as follows:

> I promise to faithfully fulfill
> all of the commitments I have made
> to myself and others.

Seth now had the last word before the participants went off to their well-deserved lunch. "Our roles as leaders are not that simple. Much of our work in today's people-centered work world involves meaning-making and promise-keeping. Filling these roles creates a soundness of character because the promises you live by are not situational but are stable. It is the most effective path to establishing our credibility with others. I believe a leader's depth of character is revealed most in their promises and their commitment to keeping them."

REVIEW

Promise-keeping represents the third and final step on the *me* path. It leverages our deepest foundation—our personal values. The challenge is that the personal values discussion is inherently difficult—mostly because our values tend to remain hidden, ambiguous, and intangible. To make this discussion workable, we substitute the word *promise* for *personal values*. The concept of a "promise" is much more user friendly than that of personal values. The reality is that we all make "promises" on a regular basis—but rarely do we spend time clarifying our "personal values." The breakthrough is to think of our values as the promises we make to ourselves and to others. Sometimes they are more implicit (hidden) than explicit (clear)—but they are still promises. In total, our promises represent our value system—creating stability and a sense of purpose that is necessary for living and leading in today's world.

REFRAME

Our reframing challenge for this chapter is best captured by John F. Kennedy's famous challenge: Ask not what your country can do for you, but ask what you can do for your country. It gets to the heart of the *me-we* journey and symbolizes the dilemma faced by Linda. Ultimately we all have to ask, What meaning do I bring to this situation? To this organization? To this relationship?

REFLECT

A promise is the most significant leadership gesture that we can make. What are the most important work-related promises that you have made? To what degree do these promises need to be better articulated or made more public?

chapter 8

From *me* to *we*

ONE THING I KNOW: THE ONLY
ONES AMONG YOU WHO WILL BE
REALLY HAPPY ARE THOSE WHO
WILL HAVE SOUGHT AND FOUND
HOW TO SERVE.

—Albert Schweitzer

Seth stepped to the front of the room and brought the room back to order. "I am inspired by the progress you have made today. We have just concluded the final step of the *me* path, and I want to give you a visual picture of our journey." Seth revealed a simple flowchart of the three steps. "The *me* path is the inner journey where we learn to become purposeful in life. It is important that you have a simple image of the critical steps. My hope is that it will serve as a mental map that will also guide you in the future.

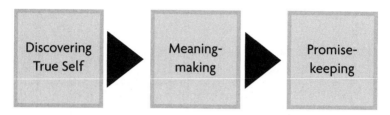

THE ME PATH. The inner journey of developing our leadership voice.

"Our journey starts with a clear sense of the self and a desire to test ourselves in the real world. Once we begin to clarify our inner strengths, it is impossible not to act on them. The second step is where we learn and create new meanings. We do this through reflection and reframing as we try to make meaningful sense out of our experience. We become energized by the process and start to form a more secure identity.

"The third step on the path, promise-keeping, is where we begin to translate our new meanings into personal values or promises that will guide our future choices. We take extra time to clarify and claim what is most important to us. By keeping our commitments and promises, a true north emerges that can bring a special quality to our lives. It compels us to continually develop and make visible an enduring set of promises that we can call our own.

"Over time, our me turns into a major force—leveraging our amazing capacity to create meaning. Our life orientation changes dramatically as well. With a life philosophy based on meaning, our defaults begin to change. Instead of protecting our fragile identities by focusing on the bad news in others, we see the good news first. Instead of reacting, we reflect. Reframing the negative becomes a natural act. We actually think more—improving our choices—instead of living from impulse to impulse.

"Now with a strong sense of self starting to take hold, life asks us one of its most important questions." Seth held up his business card and asked the same question he had asked earlier in the day. "I see whom you work for—but whom do you serve?

"Moving from *me* to *we* is the most important transition we can make as leaders. It is moving beyond the strong pull of our own success and self-interest—to service. It is a choice about how we see ourselves in relation to others. The good news is that we all have a natural need to serve—to help others—to be something beyond ourselves. It is also the critical first step on the *we* path. It can begin only with this simple but profound choice." Seth revealed the first step on a flip chart page and let the message sink in.

Step 1
The *We* Path

Choose to serve

Goal: Developing a personal orientation that
moves us from self-interest to service

"When I think of service to others, I think of my dad. For years he ran the corner grocery store. I would work there in the summers, and as a result I got to know my dad in a much deeper way. Before these experiences, I remember thinking that my dad's job wasn't very important. As kids, we'd get locked up in the comparison game, and a dad who was a small grocery store owner just didn't seem as significant as the other dads who were doctors, attorneys, or police officers.

"What I learned is that my dad made a life out of serving others. The grocery store was just a means for that service to occur. It started with his employees. They weren't just hired hands or lowly clerks but real human beings. That's what he saw first. Because they were in his employ, he felt a special responsibility to take care of them. He made sure that they were paid fairly and had the necessary health benefits. He also got to know each one of them in a very special way.

"The whole operation, although small, was built around the employees. The job assignments were crafted to what people liked to do and what they did best. Work schedules were constantly juggled to accommodate their kids' soccer matches or other special family events. There was virtually no turnover except the times when my dad would use his connections in the community to help someone advance his or her career somewhere else.

"Deep down the employees knew that my dad cared for them. Until meeting my dad, I am sure that few of them ever thought they could make a career out of being a store clerk. They repaid him with extra effort and commitment that would be uncommon for these types of service jobs.

"His customers felt the same way. In fact, this is where my dad's service ethic truly came to life. More than just being nice or friendly, he loved to take care of people.

"His first order of business was to learn someone's name. For new customers, this always caught them off guard. Not only did he want to get to know them, he wanted to serve their every need. He would make special orders for products they wanted him to carry, even if it meant surrendering some of the profits. It was amazing to see the large number of customers who made shopping at his store a daily routine.

"My dad was such a positive role model that his willingness to serve others became infectious. It was fun to watch both his employees and his customers initiate an upward spiral of positive emotions with friendly comments and chatter. Stan's Corner Grocery became much more than a place to shop.

"The family was worried when the larger food chains came in and provided pricing and selection way beyond what dad could offer. The funny thing is I don't think it ever made dad nervous. I think he knew that he was offering something that the big boys couldn't. He sold the business to his employees when he was well into his seventies. It is still operating today under the same name and same service ethic.

"I love telling that story—but now comes my first question for you. Who comes to mind when you think of service to others, and why? In your small groups, I want you to spend a few minutes identifying the role models in your life."

> Who comes to mind when you think of
> *service to others*–and why?

There was great passion in the participant voices, but reluctantly, Seth called time and brought their attention back to the front of the room. "Deep down, we all long for the leader who wants to serve us. It is not an easy thing to do. I have tried to be that leader, but I have often come up short.

"I found that the competitive realities of the business day would take my focus elsewhere. I spent my psychic energy and attention fixing problems and worrying about all of the gaps that continuously appeared." Seth paused and then rattled off a series of examples. "Sales are off. Morale is down. Our competitors are gaining share. The economy is weakening. The union is making new demands. Our customers are not happy!" Seth let his final exhortation fill the room.

"So, let's get personal here. What fills your waking moments? Problems or opportunities? The good news or the bad news? On the drive home from work each day, do you think of all the good things that went well or the two things that didn't?

> Problems
> or Opportunities?

"As leaders, we can get trapped in this deficit-based view of the world. Our best personal resources get used up in solving problems, and we fail to produce the shared vision so desperately wanted by those we serve. Problems win out over people and purpose. As a result, we fail to produce the kind of employee commitment that leads to the innovation, engagement, and the extra effort needed to win in today's world.

"That is why the choice to serve is so critical. It brings balance to the urgent and powerful draw of a problem-focused world. It also serves as an expression of who we are. As it was with my dad, it is an attitude— a way of life. It starts with the decision to lead in a fundamentally different way.

"To help you with this decision, I want to expose you to the central tension that exists between traditional leadership—the independent view—and a service orientation—the *inter*-dependent view. It is my experience that the traditional or independent view prevails in organizational life. It is characterized by self-reliance and rugged individualism. It is also fueled by the belief that through hard work we will achieve success, and many believe that by pursuing our own self-interests, the greater good for society will be achieved. On the surface, its attributes are appealing.

> # Independent View
> (Traditional Leadership)
> vs.
> # Inter-dependent View
> (Service-oriented leadership)

"The independent mindset believes that success or failure is the individual's responsibility. It also supports the most dominant image of our corporate leaders—overly independent and driven by success at any cost. However, as was the case in my life, this independence isolates us from our most powerful resources—those we serve."

Seth held up one of his business cards. "The independent view lives on the printed side of the card." Seth paused and then turned the card over revealing the blank side. "The elusive inter-dependent view of serving others is not well known in our go-go world. It is the *we*-centered view. It begins with the recognition that we are all in this together—that success is accomplished through others." Seth now revealed a flip chart page that highlighted the two themes.

Independence	Inter-dependence
"Self-centered"	"*We*-centered"
Printed side of card	The other side of the card

"Through a service mindset, the leader seeks to fully understand the needs of others—creating a larger, collective view of the desired end state. The approach is not—What can I achieve through my leadership?—but rather—What larger purpose can we achieve together? It looks beyond the heroic, independent deeds of one person to what can be achieved when the leader ventures beyond the independent to the inter-dependent.

"I want to lead you through an exercise that I hope will begin to help you see—and eventually resolve—the tensions of independence and inter-dependence on the path to serving others more fully.

"In this example, I want to show you how my dad, through his service mindset, leveraged the inter-dependent, or *we*-centered, orientation in his work and life. The answers in the far right column represent his approach—that is, how he responded to both his customers and his employees. In your small groups, I want you to do two things.

"First, I want you to review each question and discuss what you perceive to be the real differences between the independent and inter-dependent leadership mindsets. There are no right answers—it is rich dialogue that I am after. Second, I want you to discuss how you currently are answering these questions. Try to determine the degree to which you and your work group are *we*-centered in serving your customers and employees. Please begin."

My Dad	Leadership Mindset	
	Independence	Inter-dependence
	"Self-centered" Printed side of card	"*We*-centered" The other side of the card
Customers		
1. Who determines products and services?	I do, based on objective analysis	Customers do, based on their true needs
2. How do I measure success?	Profitability–how much money I make	Growth–driven by loyal customers
Employees		
1. How do I assign and schedule the work?	Based on effective human resources planning	Based on individual strengths and needs
2. How do I manage people performance?	By providing objective performance criteria	By facilitating personal growth for each person

Seth gave the group a full thirty minutes to process the exercise and then led them through a spirited post mortem. He then provided his closing comments for this section of the day. "Service to others is at the center of one of the great paradoxes in life. When you serve others as a leader, your personal capacities and resources are not lessened—they are enhanced. More influence, support, and treasure will naturally fall to those with this abundant view. However, the most wonderful benefit that befalls those who serve is the sense of grace and psychological ease they enjoy—sidestepping the normal anxiety and fear that invade our self-centered lives."

REVIEW

Moving from *me* to *we* is the most significant transition we can make in our quest to develop our personal leadership voice. It is moving beyond the strong pull of our own success and self-interest—to service. The good news is that we all have a natural need to serve others. Most important, it represents a fundamental choice in how we will lead. It is not a traditional choice that would directly proceed to an action step. Rather, it is a way of being.

REFRAME

The choice to serve represents the leader's most significant reframing challenge. It means resolving the central tension that exists between traditional leadership (the independent view) and a service-oriented leadership (the inter-dependent view). The independent view prevails in organizational life and is characterized by self-reliance and rugged individualism. It is represented by the printed side of the card. The inter-dependent view is the *we*-centered approach. It begins with the recognition that we are all in this together and that we truly exist through others. It is represented by the other side of the card—where our real work as leaders begins.

REFLECT

Think about the most important things you are trying to achieve through you leadership agenda. Which one of these goal areas would best benefit from a more *we*-centered approach?

chapter

9

They don't care what you know until they know that you care

Just one step into the *we* path and Seth realized he was leading this group into uncharted waters. He knew that developing an authentic leadership voice is a rare journey that few of us make—and fewer sustain. The reason was simple for Seth. We tend to think of leadership as something we do. To be more precise, we tend to think of it as something we do to others. Seth knew from experience that leadership in the new world had nothing to do with these things. Leadership is a relationship.

"The challenge is that our need to serve will never fully develop until we can create the capacity to care for others. It was at the core of my dad's service ethic. It also represents our next step on the *we* path. It may strike some of you as odd that I would suggest that we care for each other. Somehow, caring seems out of place for the business world where we are supposed to keep our professional distance.

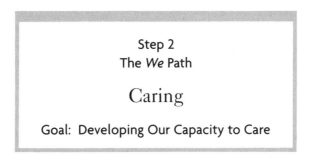

Step 2
The *We* Path

Caring

Goal: Developing Our Capacity to Care

"However, our view changes as we begin to see that we are truly connected to others. We learn that the problems of others are actually our problems too. If some of my employees are struggling because they are placed in the wrong job, then their poor performance will ultimately lower the performance of the group. We experience this same revelation over and over again as we work with teammates, partners in the organization, and our customers. Their problems are ultimately our problems. With that recognition, we begin to empathize with them—seeing the world from their perspective.

"In other words, caring is about developing a special mindfulness of others. It does not require intimacy or closeness. It is born out of respect for other people and the recognition that we are all in this together. This capacity to care—to maintain an 'others' orientation—must precede our desire to lead. Without this orientation, our leadership is not born out of the desire to help or create meaningful change—but is simply the execution of our own personal agenda. To help me make the point, I am going to ask Paul to come up again and tell his story on how he made this transition to the *we* path. Paul, the floor is yours."

"Thank you, Seth. This is my favorite story to share because I believe it tells so much about the necessary shift we have to make to see and care for others. I was making great progress on the *me* path when I got knocked off my horse. It happened on a class field trip to a museum.

"All of the eighth graders went, and so did the teachers. At lunch I sat with a handful of students from my class. There was this initial awkwardness as they started to ask me questions. It truly caught me off guard. But soon I could sense that they truly wanted to know me. The more the conversation flowed, the more I found myself really wanting to get to know them.

"I came to realize that they just weren't awkward, unfinished versions of a real person because they were in eighth grade. They were engaging, funny, and sophisticated—and they wanted to make a real connection with their math teacher. We talked about everything but math. Finally, Lena interrupted the spontaneous flow of the conversation with the following question, 'Will you be this friendly in class tomorrow?'

"Wow. She got right to the core. I fumbled a weak response, but I knew what she was really asking: '"Will we continue to get to see the real you? Can you bring more of who you really are to your teaching? Can you truly care about us?' This lunch and Lena's question put me on a new discovery path that would change my life.

"I didn't know where this would go, but I didn't want to lose the tension inspired by the question. The more I reflected on her question, the more I realized that I was too focused on my own identity as a teacher and a young professional—and that was keeping me from giving them equal status. In other words, I didn't see their humanity. I also let their youth, their immaturity, and their adolescent masks create a barrier between us. The informal lunch setting provided a glimpse of a greater potential that existed between us.

"Over the next few days, my soul searching led me to realize that I was letting my identity default to my title. In other words, what I presented and what the students saw was a dedicated teacher. I guess the image of teacher was more powerful than the image of *me* that I had developed at this point in my life. I was protecting a narrow identity, built only around my job. As a result, Mr. Jordan, the 'great' teacher, seemed to connect only with a few 'great' students, and the rest were seen as less or incomplete in some way.

"The truth was that I could hide my vulnerabilities and gain great comfort in the role of teacher. It gave me a clear script on how to look, act, and be around the students. I had it down perfect. So perfect, that I had failed to connect with most of the students. Without that connection, I wasn't able to find an entry point to get them truly excited about math. So perfect, that I wasn't able to access my best gifts.

"I want to restate what Seth said earlier. We do not exist alone—we exist through others. By creating force fields around a job-based identity and a self-centered view of the world, I was failing to fully integrate with my world. I was living only on the printed side of the card. I was also learning that it was the *we*—the ability to be in service to others—that makes the world go 'round. The *we* completes the *me*!

"As a result of this realization, I started doing things differently. I started to take down the scaffold that I had erected around *me*. I believe you will find a similar reframing challenge in your new roles. Your co-workers don't need a boss—they need someone who can truly see things from their perspective and is sincerely interested in their growth. Someone who cares.

"The first step I took was a simple one. I decided I would greet each student at the door as he or she came in each morning. I wanted the students to know that I knew their name as I locked onto them in a way that said 'I see you.' The students knew immediately that something was up, and Lena pressed me for the details by asking if this had anything to do with our lunch discussion.

"The next thing I did was to take away all of the busy work that was reinforcing my image as teacher but not really adding value. But 4he most significant thing I did was to throw away the traditional grade book and replace it with a simple binder with a tab for each student. I wasn't sure of all that would go in there, but I wanted the flexibility to make changes. Most importantly, I wanted to create a connection strategy for each student.

"My first attempts were hit and miss, but over time I created a fairly solid profile for each student. It included their strengths and weaknesses in math; their ongoing progress in the course; and a special section I called 'handle with care.' This is where I tried to capture the unique development issues at play with each student. To make the *we* work, you have to see the whole person.

"What I learned about you, Seth, was that you excelled when you got a chance to practice. In fact, I had a good number of students like you. They were bright and always understood the concepts—but they didn't own the new knowledge until they had a chance to work with it more deeply. That's why I started the 'lunch bunch.' I knew it would be tough for you to practice on your own—especially with all of your other activities and homework—so I made it fun so that you would all come."

Seth laughed out loud and Paul invited his comment. "It did feel more like fun than work. I actually thought it was cool to hang out with a teacher."

Paul smiled and continued. "Here's the other side. Making the *we* work wasn't always fun. As you know, adolescence is a trying time, and the students certainly knew how to push my buttons. I remember times when it just seemed like most of the students in the class were acting out. I simply couldn't get through to them.

"So there were days when I would temporarily give up and revert back to teacher mode. I stopped connecting and started my slow burn. I also got even!" Paul pauses and then reveals his secret. "I would assign lots of homework. It made me feel better in a not-so-good way.

"Anyway, I always would take my frustrations home with me. I remember one time my wife noticed right away. Thank God for her! She knew all about my *me-we* life philosophy, and she held me accountable to it. In fact, in many ways she knew it better than I did.

"She saw the forlorn look walking through the door and directed me immediately to the couch. I initially pretended that it was minor—just one of those bad days. But she knew better.

"She had me recount my story. With doglike eyes I talked of the immature students who were taking advantage of me and wouldn't let me teach. My soul pleaded for her recognition of how I was wronged! I completed my story, and she patiently asked if I was done. I nodded yes. Then she helped me back on the *we* path.

"She acknowledged my frustration but got right to the root cause. She felt that I valued them so deeply that I was feeling a loss of connection as they were pushing and testing their adolescent limits. Then she got very clear with me. She told me to never-ever do anything to undermine the relationships I worked so hard to develop. In other words, in my own private space, I could be disappointed, upset, and even angry. But I could never let those feelings turn into hurtful behaviors. I could never stop caring.

"I now realized that I had let the situation get the best of me. I would temporarily and emotionally sever my connection with them—seeking the protection and safety of my teacher role. I hated how I felt, but I didn't know how to reverse the cycle of doom. I would always bounce back in a day or two—but I didn't like these side tours that would take me off the *we* track.

"Here's what I learned to do. It isn't easy and takes some real resolve in the heat of the moment. The key is not to disconnect. Once we make that emotional or psychological separation from others, the downward spiral begins. We begin to lose our *we*. We can then see others only through diminished eyes. We have to in order to justify our feelings. We stop seeing their humanity. More significantly, we stop caring."

REVIEW

Moving from *me* to *we* is the most significant transition we can make as leaders in organizations. It is moving beyond the strong pull of our own success and self-interest—to service. The good news is that we all have a natural need to serve beyond ourselves. The challenge is that our capacity to serve will never fully develop until we can develop the capacity to care for others. It is a way of being more than it is a skill set. We learn that their problems are also our problems. With that recognition, we begin to empathize with others, feel for them, and are inspired to serve their needs. This is our primary work as leaders—caring for those we lead and those we serve.

REFRAME

In Paul's *we* journey, he reframed his narrow role as teacher to that of a broader, more serving role as a facilitator of potential. In our personal reframing challenge, each of us needs to assess the degree to which our role defines us (for example, I am a police officer) versus our ability to shape the role in true service to others (for example, I empower people to feel safe and secure in their communities).

REFLECT

As leaders, we learn that they don't care what you know until they know that you care. For your most important leadership mission, who are "they" and to what degree do they feel that you understand their needs?

10

In this new world, we all must lead in some way

THINGS DO NOT CHANGE.
WE CHANGE.

—Henry David Thoreau

"We have reached our final step on the *we* path. Please give yourselves a hand!" Seth led the applause—making eye contact with as many managers as possible. "Today has truly been a great opportunity for Paul and me to share the *me-we* journey. The *me* path is the inner game of discovering our unique leadership voice, and the *we* path is the leadership journey where we leverage this voice in service to others."

Seth revealed the three steps of the *we* path—showing how they complete the journey. "The *we* path is about our most important choice as leaders—the choice to serve others. The choice to serve pulls us beyond our roles in the hierarchy—where we faithfully fulfill the printed side of our card."

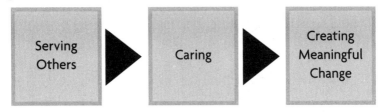

THE WE *PATH. The Outer Journey of Serving Others*

"This choice to serve also taps into our deep need to make a meaningful difference—to put ourselves into play in a world that truly needs us. Our willingness to serve, our *we*, creates a powerful new way of thinking about leadership that focuses on meaningful change as the primary pathway to bringing both integrity and credibility to our work. The creation of meaningful change does this by cutting through the challenge of organizational life by highlighting what is most important. Without this meaning—we will struggle to counteract the level of change, uncertainty, and complexity we face as leaders. I know these lessons all too well from surviving the recent downturn.

"It truly was an extraordinary time in our history. Most of you were just joining the company. There were some troubling weaknesses in the larger economy that started to put real pressure on the business. A couple of dips in profitability turned into a full-fledged downturn for Carlson. For the first time in our history, we were facing layoffs.

"We couldn't seem to stop the bleeding as we focused blindly on the urgent need of reversing our sales decline. Soon it was clear that the leadership team was lost in a frenzy to find a quick fix. Tensions were also running high throughout the organization. The first layoffs soon became a reality. The day that notices went out sent a chill through Carlson and the surrounding community. Sadness and anger were replaced by fear as we said goodbye to over 200 of our friends. It was the worst day of my life.

"To give you a feel for what it was like during this time, I wrote down the words that describe the kinds of actions and behaviors I was engaged in over those challenging two years." Seth revealed a prepared flip chart page with the following words and read each phrase out loud.

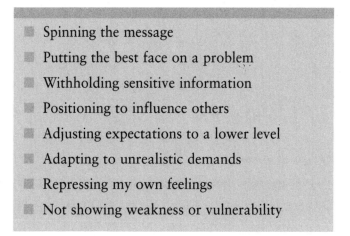

- Spinning the message
- Putting the best face on a problem
- Withholding sensitive information
- Positioning to influence others
- Adjusting expectations to a lower level
- Adapting to unrealistic demands
- Repressing my own feelings
- Not showing weakness or vulnerability

"Let's take a closer look together. These are the phrases that captured the spirit of my work. When you look at them in total, what do you see?" Seth paused for a few long moments and then continued. "They are more about compromise than true collaboration and more about positioning than purpose. They are also more about making incremental gains than meaningful progress. In short, they lack the authenticity of the meaning-making process.

"Initially, there was a sense of competence from being able to juggle the significant demands of the downturn. All eyes were on me as I commanded the ship through treacherous waters. There was a feeling of confidence that everything I had done in the past would prepare me for this challenge." Seth paused a few moments and then continued. "This time it was different.

"This time the problems were so big that it was fear—not meaning—that was claiming my psychic energy. I was steering the ship—but soon I had lost its full command. I was impatient, demanding, and over-directing. Fear had gripped the organization—and me. We started playing the smaller, survival game. We hunkered down, took small steps, and reacted without thinking. Sadly, our own selfish interests came to the forefront—fueled by the reality that our collective future with Carlson was gravely in doubt.

"The turning point for me came during a town hall meeting with our employees. We were scheduling these meetings almost monthly as a way to manage the fear that was spreading through the organization. I remember how one woman, Angie, stood and simply asked— What is our vision for the future? She was deeply frustrated by the lack of a clear game plan that kept her from playing a more meaningful role in the turnaround. She was right. She also had the courage to stand and say what many were thinking. The lonely drive home that night led to some important admissions.

"My wife, Cassie, provided a simple supper and the willingness to participate in a kitchen table post mortem. The truth was that our incremental, small-step approach was devoid of any real meaning that could pull us from our painful demise. My role had been reduced to late-night strategizing with the leadership team—that only led to more late night strategizing. Not only did we fail to provide clear direction—we left our employees waiting on the sidelines.

"Cassie was fully aware of the pressure I was under. My sleepless nights became her sleepless nights. She also knew that I was off my game—lost in a gut-wrenching effort to save the company. Her advice to me was simple. I had to start leading again." Seth paused briefly before revealing his response to Cassie's counsel. "That hurt. I was defensive at first because I truly believed that I was leading. I certainly felt responsible for getting us out of this mess." Seth walked back to the chart that revealed the true spirit of his leadership and pointed to it again.

- Spinning the message
- Putting the best face on a problem
- Withholding sensitive information
- Positioning to influence others
- Adjusting expectations to a lower level
- Adapting to unrealistic demands
- Repressing my own feelings
- Not showing weakness or vulnerability

"But this was my reality. It was painful at first—but in the safety of my own home I was starting to see that I was not leading. I was carefully managing—doing my best. But I was not leading. I had lost connection with the *me-we* philosophy that had guided me in better times. That night, in my kitchen, I made a commitment to engage the whole organization in meaningful change. It would be the only thing powerful enough to counter the fear that had captured our culture.

"Slowly but surely, I was able to regain my leadership voice. I found my neutral gear again—taking time to truly reflect on the things that mattered most. Instead of being afraid, I started caring again. I also started to lean on the relationships that had been developed over time with other Carlson leaders. As a team, we were able to create a compelling new vision for the future.

"More importantly, we were able to engage the Carlson team in creating the meaningful change that was needed to support it. We formed dozens of innovation and improvement teams. With patience and persistence, we were able to stimulate new thinking, leverage our best personal resources, and begin to reclaim a future that a few months earlier seemed hopelessly out of our reach.

"This is why I am here today. This is the message I need to deliver most. Creating meaningful change represents our final and most important step on the *we* path. It captures the essence of what it means to lead. The other five steps of the *me-we* journey are important preparations for fully developing our leadership voice. But let's be clear. Leading is creating meaningful change." Seth paused now and revealed a flip chart page with step 3.

Step 3
The *We* Path

Creating Meaningful Change

"We need to truly own this final step. Let's take a closer look at our three-word definition. *Creating* is our first word. The act of creating gets at the larger domain that leaders operate in. They don't just command—they facilitate, bring to life, make new, inspire, and build.

"The second word is *meaningful*—the central theme of today's journey. To be meaningful, the change we seek is in service to something beyond ourselves. It reflects our capacity to care and represents the collective needs of those we are connected to.

"The third and final word is *change*. Change is inevitable. Meaningful change is not. The change we seek emphasizes our choice to serve others. The key word in this three-word definition is *meaningful*. Change that isn't meaningful just won't capture the hearts of those who must fulfill our work missions.

"Creating meaningful change is the right answer. It elevates our status in a transactional world. It seeks alignment with our most important purposes. It reduces the rationalizations that can head us down the wrong path. It attaches the change agenda to something larger than our own narrow self-interests. It is the only thing that can get us past the fear. The meaningful nature of our work now has the potential to transform us, to make us better.

"This kind of discussion may sound too abstract or too soft to apply in the 'real world.' But the reality is that we won't be able to reach our potential or maximize our performance opportunities until we feel we are serving worthwhile purposes. Without attaching ourselves to a meaningful purpose, we won't be able to move beyond the shallow nature that characterizes much of our work and our relationships to others. Success and prosperity will always be fleeting unless they are linked to meaningful change.

"I have an exercise that I hope will create a useful framework for developing your meaningful-change agenda. I hope it will help you to move some of what you learned today into action. Let's get started.

"Take out three business cards and draw a line down the center of each one. In the left-hand box, write the label 'Current Problem.' In the right-hand box, write the label 'Meaningful Change.' It should look like this." Seth now held up a business card and walked the room for everyone to see.

Current Problem	Meaningful Change

"OK, now comes the important question. Which box do we complete first? In other words, do we work from left to right—identifying our most important problems first? Or do we work from right to left—starting with the meaningful change we seek?" Seth gave them a few seconds to ponder—but he could see from their confident smiles that they knew. "The answer please!" The managers responded—almost in unison— "You start from the right!"

"You are too good. As leaders we intuitively know this to be true. But let's explore why." Seth paused to underscore the importance of the discussion. "As we discussed before, much of the work we do is problem-focused. In fact, the majority of our days revolve around solving problems.

"But here's the deal. If the starting point is always the problem, then it is the scope of the problem that will define the scope of the solution. In other words, we will unwittingly limit the meaningful change we can create if we cannot move beyond the urgency of our current problems and challenges.

"The real work of leaders is to carve out time to start with the meaningful change that we seek. For the moment, we suspend our attention on what is wrong. We move beyond the narrow focus of the pain that we are feeling in our organizations. We move from right to left. We define the meaningful change that is worthy of our collective commitment. Inevitably it will solve the problems that confront us."

Seth once again paused to let the message sink in. "Let's begin to build our leadership agenda for the future. Begin by describing three meaningful changes that are worthy of your commitment. After you have done so, move to the left box and try to identify some of the current problems in your organization that the meaningful change will address." Seth monitored the progress and then led the group in an engaging debriefing. Dan Anderson from marketing volunteered to share one of his examples—which he captured on a flip chart page for everyone to see.

Current Problem	Meaningful Change
▪ Lack of clear vision	▪ Create a compelling brand promise that serves the true needs of our customers
▪ Fragmented work	
▪ No service ethic	

Dan's intent was clear, but Seth asked for an explanation from the young manager. Dan stood and delivered: "I loved the exercise because it gave me a chance to get some of my big ideas on the table. Although we do a good job of promoting our products and services, I have always felt that we could lift our game by creating a customer-centered promise that we all would commit to. The hope is that it would create absolute clarity on how our products and services would serve their true needs. It would also be a promise that would differentiate us—a pledge that would be unique to Carlson.

"I also believe it would help us to solve some of the current problems that have been weighting us down. Let me explain the third one I have listed"—no service ethic. What I mean is that most of us in the marketing department do not come into contact with customers. As a result, I think we have lost touch with their real needs. Our desire to be creative is overshadowing our need to serve. For example, sometimes our energy gets lost in creating a cool promotion that will impress our colleagues—with our customers nowhere in view. A clear and compelling promise—focused on real people—could bring meaning and value to our work."

REVIEW

The last step of the journey is where we activate our leadership voice. It is where we put it all together—and more importantly—put ourselves into play in a world that truly needs us. Our willingness to serve, our *we*, creates a powerful new way of thinking about leadership that focuses on meaningful change as the primary pathway to bringing both integrity and credibility to our work. In the process of creating meaningful change, we not only become more aware of our personal and collective power—we begin to see opportunities that we could not have seen before. Creating meaningful change captures the essence of what it means to lead.

REFRAME

The reality is that much of the work we do is problem-focused. To a large degree, it defines our day. Here's the dilemma: If the starting point is always the problem—then the scope of the problem will also define the scope of the solution. We will limit the meaningful change we can create if we cannot move beyond the urgency of our current problems and challenges.

REFLECT

This is the most important question that you as leaders need to answer—continuously! What is the meaningful change that you seek?

chapter 11

The other side of the card is where you will find *me* and *we*

DESTINY IS NOT A MATTER OF
CHANCE, IT IS A MATTER OF
CHOICE; IT IS NOT A THING TO BE
WAITED FOR, IT IS A THING TO BE
ACHIEVED.

—William Jennings Bryan

Seth had reached the end of day. There was only one exercise left, and the rest was ceremonial. The evening would conclude with a special celebration dinner and a final opportunity to get the voices of these future leaders into the room. Seth's assistant, Jane, handed each one the address for the Lakeside Inn. Seth then gave the final instructions.

"We will meet at the inn for a well-deserved reception and dinner. Your enthusiastic and passionate participation has been inspiring. Carlson is lucky to have you as the newest members of the leadership team!" Seth led them in congratulatory applause before making a final request. "I need you to do one more thing before we depart.

"Here is your last challenge. In a single day we have explored the *me* and *we* paths that represent lifetime journeys that are elusive by their nature. To achieve this impossible task, it was important to break these paths down into understandable and digestible steps. You have done a phenomenal job of working through the exercises that represent each of the steps on the journey. But now we need to put it all back together in a meaningful way. One of the most powerful ways to capture learning for both ourselves and others is through storytelling.

"You have heard over a dozen leadership stories today. We believe it is one of the most important skills that a leader can develop. Long before there were books, there were stories. This narrative form of communication has been hard-wired into our brains through the evolution of humanity. It is the form of learning that we assimilate best—bringing credibility to information by attaching it to a human voice. I have a great example.

"About two years ago, I sat on the board for our local homeless shelter. All of our fundraising efforts to support our various programs had stalled. We found that there was a basic belief in the community that it was the homeless who were committing a large number of crimes. This was due to a few highly sensationalized incidents. As a result, people could not identify with our cause. All of our efforts to paint a different picture with the facts were fruitless.

"By accident, we found our breakthrough. A fellow board member was Pastor James Mann. In a Sunday sermon he featured one of our homeless clients, Davie, as a speaker. Davie simply told his story of decline that began with the loss of both of his parents in high school. He actually got within a few credits of graduating from college before his problems became complicated with a burglary conviction. His downward spiral became his life as he battled drug and alcohol dependency for over thirty years.

"The parishioners sat in rapt silence as his tale of woe unfolded—no family, no friends, no options for a meaningful life. He had painted the darkest picture of despair that most had ever heard. Then the clouds started to part as Davie told how one of our outreach counselors, Jan, had finally broken through.

"She simply would not give up on him—treating him with respect that he had not witnessed in years. Over time he developed the conviction to not let her down. As a result, he had been drug and alcohol free for nine months. He performed building maintenance work for three different churches—earning his first paycheck at the age of forty-seven. He gained his paying jobs by first volunteering and earning the trust and respect of his employers.

"He also described a new-found self-esteem that had otherwise eluded him for most of his life. But his final words were about his deep and profound gratitude to Jan for the opportunity to turn his life around. Some were brought to tears by this remarkable story of how the human spirit can prevail. The offering basket over-flowed with generosity.

"It is now our common practice to put real people up in front of the community to tell their true story. We stopped trying to counter perceptions with data only. We put a face on it. The face tells a real story that cre-ates a human connection that is far more powerful than statistical data.

"We tend to discount storytelling in our organiza-tional lives because we believe hard facts and rational thinking are more valuable. That's unfortunate. As I mentioned earlier, people don't care what you know until they know that you care. Before you capture their minds, you need to win their hearts. The best way to get to the heart is through an emotional connection.

"There is one important thing to remember as you develop your stories. People relate best to people—not concepts. More than a presentation, we want a story that features real people and real issues. A presentation proceeds rationally, but a story locks us in emotionally because we can identify with the human qualities that emerge. Paul didn't make a presentation today—he told stories.

"Now it is your turn. Like many of the other exercises today, the thirty minutes I will give you is just enough to see the power behind the process. Believe me, it will take a lot more practice to fully develop your storytelling capabilities. But it will become easier as you continue to build your life stories—and tell many of them over and over again.

"To fully engage your leadership voice, I want you to capture one of the most significant events of your emerging leadership journey and prepare to tell it in the most compelling way. Limit this first story to five minutes. It has to meet only two criteria: It has to be about you, and it has to make a meaningful point. Just like Davie's story did. Later tonight, I will give you an opportunity to tell your story in small groups."

The next hour quickly evaporated. In small groups, the managers began to arrive at the inn. Seth and Paul were waiting to greet each one as they entered the great room. The view of the lake as the daylight faded was magnificent—drawing all eyes to the window. The fire was blazing—and the natural light of the candles created a special glow that illuminated all that was good in each face. It was the perfect setting to end the day.

The reception chatter continued to grow until the hostess of the inn made the call for dinner. Seth provided his welcoming comments and toasted the new managers, officially welcoming them to Carlson's leadership ranks. The day had been a remarkable journey for all involved.

As the dessert plates were cleared, he invited them back into the great room to share their stories. They all settled into the deep couches and chairs. "Before I turn it over to you, I'd like to tell one last story.

"It will help me to complete some of the stories I started today. It will also allow me to reach closure on what has been a challenging chapter in my life. It started with surviving a business downturn that pushed us to the brink. Unknowingly, I had fallen off the *me-we* journey, and the downturn was a wake-up call to reclaim the leadership voice that Paul had helped me to develop earlier in my career.

"Believe it or not, things actually got more challenging for me during this last year when I started my transition role—easing into retirement. It was supposed to be a victory lap of sorts—a chance to enjoy the successes of a career of more than forty years. But with the transfer of responsibility, I felt as though I had been taken out of the game. For the first time in my work life, I felt irrelevant.

"The abundance of reflective moments that I had during this time of transition, awakened some of the deeper lessons I had learned in both a career and a life. I had to speak to them. What I discovered is that I needed to take the *me-we* journey to another level of understanding—for both you and me. Without trivializing this powerful and profound philosophy, I wanted to establish clear markers on the journey. These markers are represented by the three steps on each path.

"As you know, it all begins with a strong sense of the true self. We simply cannot grow in the right directions without knowing our gifts. Through the three steps of discovering our true selves, meaning-making, and promise-keeping, we begin to establish our purpose in life. As we discovered throughout the day, each step plays a critical role in countering the powerful forces that can limit the impact of our individual lives.

"With a strong sense of purpose emerging, we have the newfound capacity to create meaning beyond ourselves. We learn that a successful career cannot sustain us unless it serves the larger needs of those we are connected to in this life. On the *we* path we develop a sincere and empathic orientation to others—creating the capacities to serve others and care deeply. The final step on the we path, creating meaningful change, is the most powerful. It is where our leadership voice fully leverages the personal and collective resources gained on the *me-we* journey to become a true force of positive change and service for the world."

Seth held his own card up and showed the printed side. "The title reads 'Chief Executive Officer.' As big as that title is, it seems insignificant in relation to all of the meaning of the *me-we* journey that we have discovered today. I hope you feel the same way."

Seth held up his CEO card one more time and revealed the backside. It was no longer blank. Written on the back was one word. The managers all leaned in, trying to make out the handful of letters. "This is where my *me-we* journey has now led me." Seth revealed the single word: "Coach."

He paused and then explained: "I want to be your coach. I have six months left on my transition assignment. I will dedicate them to you. After all, we're just getting started. I truly believe that my most important accomplishments will come at the hands—or should I say hearts—of those of you in this room."

The managers stood to give Seth an impassioned standing ovation. Today had been a life-changing experience for all participants, but it was Seth's skillful mentoring that they were acknowledging. They arrived in the morning prepared for an orientation to their new jobs as managers. Instead, they engaged in discussion that had launched them on a lifetime journey to develop their leadership voice.

Seth responded, "Thank you so much. Now we have some stories to tell! Please enjoy the fire and each other. When the final story is told, you are free to leave." Seth led one more round of applause for all of the participants. With great anticipation, the managers begin sharing their life stories.

Seth and Paul moved to the two vacant chairs near the fire. As an early riser, it was well past Paul's bedtime, but he could not resist being a part of this wonderful moment. It took only a few minutes to complete their post mortem for the day.

"Thank you again, Paul. Having you here was special for me and our young managers." Paul was humbled by the comments. After making an awkward acknowledgment, he pulled out a piece of notebook paper that had been folded neatly into fours. He handed it to Seth. As he opened it up, it only took a few seconds for Seth to recognize that this was his writing. It was a note that he had written to Paul in eighth grade.

Dear Mr. Conrad:

I want you to know how much of an impact that you have had on my life. I was just an average student until I met you. Not only did you get me excited about math, but also you got me interested in being a good student. This is the highest GPA that I have ever had in my life. More importantly, you have helped me become a better person.

I will miss the lunches and your class next year. High school should be great but I wish you were there to help us along. I hope you don't mind if I stay in contact with you.

Many thanks and have a great summer,

Seth

Seth sat back in his chair and enjoyed the rush of warm feelings from reading the letter. Paul turned to him, "Seth, this letter has always served as a special reminder to me about the significance of achieving the *we* in life. Discovering my purpose—my passion for teaching math—was not complete until I connected it to something larger than myself. You were acknowledging this connection in your note.

"If you look closely, you'll see that the note was not about me being a great teacher but about the transformation that you made. If you remember, I struggled as a young teacher, with my purpose stuck in the *me*. At first it was my insecurity as a new teacher. I found great comfort and protection in the teacher role, but it also kept me from fully connecting with the students. It was at that memorable lunch with the students—where we let our guard down—that I started to see a much bigger game evolving.

"I learned that my purpose was to look for and develop the full learning potential in students. When I started to fully connect with them, magical things happened. It transformed me. It transformed them. In the end, it made me a much better teacher. Our math scores were the highest in the state—but that was never the goal.

"I have had a lot of great students, but you kept coming back to me, Seth. You asked me to be involved in your life. It made me feel that I was on the right track with my own *me-we* journey." Paul placed his hand over his heart. "You have always given me credit for changing your life—but it was you who changed mine."

WE NEVER GET TO THE BOTTOM OF
OURSELVES ON OUR OWN. WE
DISCOVER WHO WE ARE FACE TO
FACE AND SIDE BY SIDE WITH
OTHERS IN WORK, LOVE, AND
LEARNING.

—Robert Bellah

As leaders, we pursue meaning in a never-ending conversation we have with ourselves over a lifetime. The clarity, constancy, and courage reflected in these internal conversations will be critical to creating a meaningful life for ourselves and others. As in any journey, each step we take brings a sense of anticipation, renewal, and fulfillment.

As we are able to make small steps on the *me-we* journey, we are rewarded with a deep sense of participation that can help us overcome the powerlessness that people often feel in life. We increasingly learn more about ourselves from each experience, and our confidence grows as we lean into our challenges. Most importantly, we make significant progress in achieving the personal differentiation (I know who I am) and the integration with others (I have found my place in the world) that represent the *me* and *we* paths of leadership (see the appendix for a complete description of the process).

You have the opportunity to choose the path you will take in life. I deeply believe that the best we can do as leaders is to consistently choose the path of service. Serving others, caring, and creating meaningful change will always connect us—and those we serve—to something larger than ourselves.

As do other people whose lives rest on spiritual foundations, I also believe that the meaning we create has the power to transcend our earth-bound limitations. This lifelong leadership journey stimulates many questions. What will it be like at the end? What answers will come? What sense of satisfaction can we anticipate? What level of consciousness will I have when my physical vessel finally succumbs?

I'm not sure of the answers, but I do believe that our lives can produce an abundance of positive outcomes that will allow us to live on forever. I hope to see you on the journey.

—Mike Morrison

Reframing the Personal Quest to Lead

The *Me* Path:
The Inner Journey of Developing Our Leadership Voice

1. *Discover your true self*—so that you can lead from your center of personal power.

2. *Leverage the meaning-making process*—enhancing the quality of your thinking through reflection and reframing.

3. *Highlight what is most important through promise-keeping*—elevating the status of your leadership work.

The *We* Path:
The Outer Journey of Serving Others

4. *Make the choice to serve*—creating a powerful way of being that moves us from self-interest to service.

5. *Develop the capacity to care*—engaging a special mindfulness toward others.

6. *Create meaningful change*—focusing on the true work of leadership.

Mike Morrison has been a student of leadership for as long as he can remember. One of his life goals is to help others leverage their leadership voice. As the vice president of a major corporate university, Mike gets to live his dream on a daily basis. He is also engaged in global leadership development initiatives to advance new ways of leading and thinking that promote peace and prosperity. He has a B.A. from Gonzaga University, an M.B.A. from the University of Southern California, and a Ph.D. from Claremont Graduate University. Mike lives in Los Angeles with his wife Kerry, son Zack, daughter Mackenzie, and their two Schipperkes, Kane and Addy.

Develop the
Other Side
of "Your" Card!

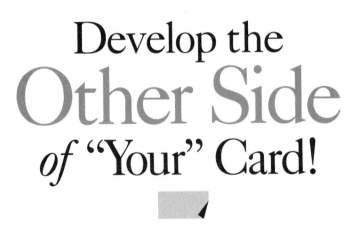

Dear Fellow Leader:

Our journey together will hopefully not end with the book. I have spent a lifetime decoding the pathway to bringing passion, power, and meaning to our personal leadership voices. I can guarantee you that success and satisfaction in life will always be elusive until you can define the other side of *your* card.

At the center of the challenge are a handful of timeless questions that must be answered and confirmed continuously. I would like to be your coach in a journey to provide responses that will be meaningful to you. To that end, I have designed a series of free support tools that you can begin to access today.

WEEKLY E-COACHING: My coaching e-letter will come to you directly each week. It will provide inspiring insights, ground level strategies and practical tips that will bring power and meaning to your personal leadership voice.

FREE DOWNLOADS: I will provide you with a series of opportunities that will help you translate ideas from *The Other Side of the Card* into meaningful change:

> **PRINT:** I will provide a wide range of practical leadership development guides that you can download. The first offering is an exciting 23-page "icebreaker and exercise" guide. From discovering the true self to creating meaningful change—these "mini" interventions are designed to help you unleash the leader in all of us.

> **AUDIO:** I will share more inspiring examples of "leading through meaning" with carefully crafted narratives, offered in two popular formats (MP3 and Windows Media .wmf).

INTERACTION OPPORTUNITIES: I plan to keep the dialogue going by responding to your questions and ideas through e-mail and creating active online forums for sharing insights with a larger community of leaders like yourself.

I look forward to our time together. Login today at:

www.theothersideofthecard.com

My best to you,

Mike Morrison